Forrest Rose
A Life in Words and Music

Cover:
Never missing an opportunity to seize the moment, Forrest hams it up in the Columbia Daily Tribune *newsroom in 1984. A column about Wal-Mart frames the photo. Preferring a pen to a keyboard for his first drafts, Forrest usually wrote his Tuesday columns on Sunday evenings from the comfort of his big easy chair.*

Inside front and back covers:
Except for the high-school rendition of William Shakespeare, all the doodles are by-products of Tuesday morning meetings in the Extension and Agricultural Information office at the University of Missouri, where he was a writer.

Forrest Rose
A Life in Words and Music
Select Columns and Songs

Edited by
Bernadette Dryden and Carol Rose

Published by Earl and Marilyn Rose
Iowa City, Iowa

Forrest Rose: A Life in Words and Music

Earl and Marilyn Rose, publishers
Iowa City, Iowa

Library of Congress Control Number: 2006906145
ISBN: 0-9786402-0-9

Printed in the United States of America

For book ordering information, please contact:
buonappetito@centurytel.net

Carol Rose, columns editor
Bernadette Dryden, general editor and project manager
Les Fortenberry, designer
Jim Curley, photographer—except where noted

Typefaces: Goudy Old Style and Myriad
Paper: Glatfelter Natural Text
Printer and binder: Walsworth Publishing Co., Marceline, Mo.

*His first column portrait for the
newspaper in 1985*

*This book is dedicated to Forrest's family, friends and fans,
who inspired his writing and music throughout the years.*

Joe Edens

On a poker table that once belonged to Harry Truman, Forrest and his parents play a hand. As a result of a browse through the classified ads, some fine sleuthing and garage-sale haggling, Forrest bagged the table for $5. He gave it to his parents the following Christmas.

Foreword

FORREST ROSE, OUR ONLY SON AND THIRD-BORN IN A FAMILY OF SIX, DIED
suddenly and unexpectedly on March 20, 2005. His life was one to celebrate.
Through his music, his relationships and his writings he made an impact on the
world about him.

This collection is a representative sampling of his many columns published
in the *Columbia Daily Tribune*, where he was encouraged and supported by
publisher Hank Waters III and managing editor Jim Robertson.

With flair, Forrest thoughtfully captured the tensions between liberal
and conservative, between equality and inequality, between discrimination
and tolerance, and between hypocrisy and honesty. His dexterous use of the
English language gracefully carried forward his thoughts with wit and clarity.
He loved to walk with his fellow men and women, but was often curiously
and challengingly out of step. Always respectful of another's ideas, he sought
to persuade, not argue. There is a timelessness to his writings, for he touched
on the universal experiences of his readers. It is these qualities that we seek to
preserve in this collection.

Hundreds came to Forrest's memorial service and celebration of his life in
Columbia. Many identified themselves to us as "Forrest's friends." He left a
wide circle of acquaintances, readers, fellow musicians, writers and people he
loved—especially his son, Brennan. Although Forrest was not present that
night, his presence was felt, just as his presence is in these selected columns.

We are indebted to Jim Curley—Forrest's longtime close friend and
colleague—who documented throughout the years, with his sensitive and
beautiful photographs, the many important moments in Forrest's life.

We thank Forrest's sister, Carol, and his beloved Bernadette for their labor
of love in compiling, editing and designing this tribute to Forrest Rose.

—His parents,
Earl and Marilyn Rose

Contents

A LIFE IN WORDS

CHAPTER 1 ON FREEDOM AND CIVIL LIBERTIES

Spies in the stacks, or the Bobbsey twins meet the FBI   2

'Rum and Coca-Cola' indeed! Ban those Andrews Sisters!   4

Parents' moral outrage is a catalyst for preteen curiosity   6

Even ignorant racists have guarantee of free speech   8

Heterosexuals are source of problems in military   10

Flag desecration debate wears out faint-of-heart   12

'School choice' is no choice for majority of Americans   14

Bad boys wear black, or druggies with buggies   16

PETA rhetoric makes fishing sound exciting   18

Bush proposes 'partnership' for fox, hens   20

Watergate showed pitfalls of secrecy   22

Flag pledge becomes meaningless chant   24

ACLU: not just for liberals anymore   26

Defend marriage one couple at a time   28

Let's shut down the abortion clinics   30

Public defenders chronically under-funded   32

Smoking ban smacks of Puritanism   34

CHAPTER 2 RELIGIOUS PURSUITS

Attacks on Halloween scarier than the holiday   38

Christians can't complain about treatment in America   40

Ask Falwell: What would Jesus do?   42

'Design' law debases science and religion   44

What kinds of Christians are these?   46

Virgin Mary, the grill of my dreams   48

There's no piety deficit in U.S. politics   50

Neither science nor faith answers the ultimate question   52

CHAPTER 3 NOTES ON MUSIC AND SOCIETY

Fiddlin' around on stage offers fix for bass junkie   56

Simulation stimulation is the brain wave of the future   58

Humor, like art, is in the eye of the beholder   60

Musical revisionism strikes a false note   62

Dress codes' dictates can't halt fashion trend   64

Society take notice: Women have lock on genetic codes   66

MU artist's work at fair misunderstood by officials   68

Bluegrass father Bill Monroe took love for music to grave   70

HMO refuses to cover cost of artificial ardor   72

Kaul, last of the liberals, inspired fledgling pundit   74

Massage wasted on spa-resistant man   76

CHAPTER 4 DISPATCHES FROM THE HOME FRONT

Nightmarish memories of a Mennonite prom   80

The most important rule in childbirth: Keep breathing   82

'The Sortin' Life,' or 'I've Got Plenty of Laundry'   84

Dear Mom: Weather's fine, and brother is under arrest   86

Some Christmas inspiration from a genuine living doll   88

Profiles in cowardice, or Don't cross that line!   90

Columnist's father heroic in assassination aftermath   92

Political slogans irrelevant to pursuit of real values   94

Clumsy dad carves niche in finger, scouting history   96

How we spent our savings on summer vacation   98

Photos can document fashion faux pas   100

All balled up by Christmas conflicts   102

CHAPTER 5 ABOUT TOWN

City pot-arrest crackdown needs healthy public debate   106

Rowdy fraternity parties belong back in Greektown   108

Mommy, what's that bronze man doing?   110

Twenty years later, kids, this Note's for you   112

Deposit law unmourned—for now   114

30-foot sticker could save 'Tiger Spot'   116

Columbia: Where the slogan goes on and on   118

Air-show arrest flips finger at 'freedom'   120

What's Wal-Mart done for us lately?   122

Wal-Mart rant was nothing personal   124

Embarrassment is a fair price to pay   126

Trolley-bus idea reeks of faux-thenticity   128

Chapter 6 America goes to war

Terrorist crimes call for justice, not war   132

Let's not fall for Bush's bait-and-switch   134

War on Iraq opens gate to mischief   136

'Peace and goodwill' more than a slogan   138

Should U.S. cut the French connection?   140

Bush fibs set bad example for children   142

Success hard to judge in murky mission   144

Good intentions paved the way to war   146

Prisoner abuse: It's the war, stupid!   148

Partisan 'truth' irrelevant in face of war   150

Iraq elections offer hope, not guarantee   152

Chapter 7 The last word

Is moral relativism ever OK?   156

Forgotten lessons of the 20th century   158

A LIFE IN MUSIC

A Life In Love With Music   162

A Life In Music 1971-2005   164

Acknowledgments   167

FORREST ROSE A Life In Music   168

A LIFE IN WORDS

Think your vote doesn't mean anything?
Try writing a weekly newspaper column!
You spend agonizing hours wringing your
soul all over the page, working out thoughtful
themes and irrefutable arguments—and nothing happens.

—Forrest Rose

When an honest writer discovers an imposition it is his
simple duty to strip it bare and hurl it down from its place
of honor, no matter who suffers by it; any other course
would render him unworthy of the public confidence.

—Mark Twain

Photographer Jim Curley and Forrest strike a 1986-style pose of "American Gothic" in front of the house in Eldon, Iowa, made famous by artist Grant Wood. About halfway between Columbia and the Rose family home in Iowa City, the house was a favorite stopover for Forrest when taking first-time visitors to his boyhood home.

CHAPTER 1

ON FREEDOM AND CIVIL LIBERTIES

Spies in the stacks, or the Bobbsey twins meet the FBI

ONE DAY LAST WEEK, IN A FIT OF LITERARY AMBITION, I REPAIRED TO A LOCAL library to indulge myself in the classics.

I had just settled myself at a library table and opened one of the great works when I noticed a fleshy figure in a gray suit peering furtively around the stacks. I attempted successfully to ignore him, and soon I was swept away on waves of rapturous prose.

Then, I heard a rustle behind me and turned to find myself at eye-level with a U.S. flag pin on a gray lapel. The mystery man had been peeking over my shoulder. Though flustered, he recovered and said, "Hey, sport. Whatcha reading?"

With icy sang-froid, I closed the book to reveal its cover. The gray-suited man started. "'Bobbsey Twins Secret at the Seashore,' eh?" he asked. "Say, is Bobbsey some kind of East European name, or what?" I leveled a retort that froze him in his wingtips and left him in the library with a red face and quivering hands.

It was only when I read a headline in last week's newspaper that I realized what had gone down in the reading room. It read: "FBI Spies on Library Patrons."

The Washington Post story reported that FBI agents have recently appeared at libraries and demanded information about the reading habits of individuals with "East European- or Russian-sounding names."

The bureau believes that foreign envoys are obtaining valuable information about U.S. technology from unclassified publications readily available in public libraries. The FBI also says libraries are prime recruiting spots for hostile espionage networks.

Herbert Foerstel, a librarian at the University of Maryland, called the program "a clumsy attempt" to force librarians "to break local laws protecting the confidentiality of library users over information that is available to anyone in the country."

California congressman Don Edwards, chairman of the House sub-committee on civil and constitutional rights, said he would be "frightened if I was afraid the librarians would report me to the FBI for reading a particular book. Anything that chills the desire, the interest of Americans in going into libraries is a very serious matter."

Assistant FBI director Thomas DuHadway tried to calm such weak-kneed liberal queasiness with a speech to the National Commission on Libraries and Informational Sciences. "We don't want you to be a spy," he said. "You're not trained to be a spy." But he cautioned, "You should know, you could be an individual target of a recruitment."

He found some support from the commission. Chairman Jerald Newman, who is not a librarian, said the program merely called on libraries to recognize "a higher responsibility" of "upholding the Constitution and that includes citizens protecting our democracy and our republic."

Librarians were quick to point out that laws in 32 states protect the confidentiality of public library borrowing. "I don't really see how a free society is able to say that journals have to be hidden from people with foreign-sounding names," Foerstel said.

My suspicions were confirmed on my next trip to the library. Ahead of me in line, an individual wearing a trench coat and fedora and carrying a bowling ball with a fuse in it was checking out "Bobbsey Twins Mystery of the Laughing Dinosaur."

I thought about reporting him, but I kept my mouth shut instead. After all, I've got a higher responsibility.

'Rum and Coca-Cola' indeed! Ban those Andrews Sisters!

IN VIGOROUS PURSUIT OF PURER PUBLIC MORALS, A MISSOURI LEGISLATOR HAS introduced a bill that would require warning labels on certain popular records and tapes.

Rep. Jean Dixon, R-Springfield, wants to label records that "may contain explicit lyrics descriptive of or advocating" a whole host of sins, including nudity, adultery, suicide, "deviant" sex, murder and "the use or illegal use of drugs and alcohol."

The reason behind the bill is, of course, to prevent children from buying albums that might lead them astray. I was about to dismiss the proposal as just another teen-harassment measure when I realized that the categories would cover a lot of the platters in my personal album collection.

Make no mistake: I would sooner do without tunes altogether than subject my ears to the likes of Slayer or Megadeath. In fact, I buy very few albums recorded after 1960. But a lot of those oldies are highly "descriptive" of—if not outright "advocating"—the sins listed in the proposed statute. Face it, "Frankie and Johnny" covers four or five areas all by itself.

Good ol' "Tom Dooley," not usually thought of as a perverse song, explicitly describes a murder, and it pales in comparison to other traditional ballads such as "Knoxville Girl." Listen to the truly macabre "Two Sisters," in which the miller fished the victim from the river and "made fiddle screws of her little finger bones." Brrr.

Suicide is also a common theme in traditional music, as in:
"She picked up the silver dagger
And plunged it through her lily-white breast
Saying 'Goodbye, Mama; Goodbye Papa,
I'll join the one I love the best.'"

A sizable portion of the older jazz and swing catalog would fall under the drug-use provision. Early jazz artists and jitterbuggers delighted in joking references to "reefer." For instance, Julia Lee in "The Spinach Song," confesses: "I didn't like it the first time, but oh, how it grew on me."

The bill's alcohol and adultery clauses cover a good third of the standard blues repertoire and nearly every cut in that venerable category known as honky-tonk music. For example, Hank Thompson's classic "Slippin' Around" and Sonny Boy Williamson's take of "One Way Out" are out-and-out cheating songs. When Big Walter Horton sang "Sloppy Drunk," he probably had no idea of the danger it posed to future generations. Roger Miller thought he'd just written a cute song in "Chug-a-lug," not created a musical menace.

An exaggeration? Listen to what Rep. Dixon said the other day in an interview on National Public Radio: "Heavy metal and rap are the worst offenders, but country music is fast getting there. There are a few of Willie Nelson's that we could put labels on."

As for "deviant" sex, the raunchy recordings of Memphis Minnie would surely demand warning labels, as would much of Bessie Smith's earlier material.

Let's hope such hair-splitting is left up to someone other than the Right Hon. Rep. Dixon. Earlier this month, Dixon told the Columbia Missourian her attitude about sexual assaults. "I hate to admit it," she said, "but young girls, by their dress and their attitudes, really ask for that to happen."

As for the men, "Gosh, you can't blame a guy—that's their chemical makeup, their gender. They're sexually motivated by sight."

This is not the person whom we want to decide what is normal sex and what is not. Dixon claimed her remarks were taken out of context, though I have trouble thinking up a context in which they don't sound ignorant and stupid. I wonder if it ever occurs to her that song lyrics have a context, too.

Apparently not. On a standard long-playing record album, Dixon would demand a fluorescent yellow label with the words: "Warning" and "Parental Advisory" in black type bigger than that of most newspaper headlines. In smaller print, the labels would list the nefarious categories and warn that the album "may contain" lyrics about them.

The bill would also require phonograph records that might offend to display their lyrics prominently on the outside of the package.

Dixon ignores a basic fact about child psychology: Any kids who want to cop an attitude—and there are plenty—feel compelled to buy the albums their mothers always warned them about. The labels—not to mention the prominently displayed lyrics—would merely make it more convenient to select the nastiest and most gruesome records in the inventory.

There's a more time-honored way of dealing with the problem of offensive music, usually involving a spoken, rather than written, parental admonition. Couched in all capital letters with an exclamation point at the end, it goes: "TAKE THAT GARBAGE OFF!" For other, less blatant recordings, the parent may modify the warning to: "TURN THAT GARBAGE DOWN!"

On the other hand, Dixon's bill might lead some of these punks to discover a whole slough of pretty good music. The material's dated, but it retains much of its original immorality.

Parents' moral outrage is a catalyst for preteen curiosity

CONCERNED CITIZENS ROUTINELY TAKE A MOMENT TO WRING THEIR HANDS EVERY time a new study informs them that the typical sixth-grader cannot point out the Aral Sea on a map of the world. The study usually reports that Japanese schoolchildren are pointing out the Aral Sea every day, which must tell us something.

Because it's important for U.S. kids to keep current, the local PTA City Council has decided not to seek the removal of Columbia's award-winning daily afternoon newspaper from public school classrooms.

Linda Poehlmann, a former PTA council president, wanted the Tribune banished from Columbia Public Schools because the newspaper has been running an advertisement for homosexual encounters. The ad promised "Man-to-man contacts" and "talking personal ads arranged by area code." There was a picture of a bare-chested young man pouting into a telephone receiver and—this is the bad part—a 900 number you could call to "meet men in your area."

The Tribune distributes 500 free papers every day to Columbia public schools, and they are used mostly in sixth-grade classes.

"That's the age of curiosity," Poehlmann said darkly, conjuring up images of 11-year-old boys plotting secret trysts with faceless pederasts. It's a terrible thought, and I can see Poehlmann's point.

I once objected to a Tribune advertisement—a classified item aiming to recruit new members for the Ku Klux Klan. I was uncomfortable that that Klan was essentially paying a small portion of my small salary.

The Tribune's management gave me essentially the same line they gave Poehlmann: The newspaper cannot fairly deny access to anyone who wants to pay the rates, even when the advertiser is a lunatic.

Did I resign in righteous indignation? No. Did I tear my paycheck into tiny pieces in an act of protest and fling the confetti in the business manager's face? Emphatically, no.

The more I thought it over, the more I agreed that even kooks and crazies ought not to be shut off. A newspaper should reflect the community as accurately as it can, and most communities have both gays and bigots.

In fairness, Poehlmann was not objecting so much to the homosexual lonely-hearts ads as she was to giving children access to the 900 number. When she raised a public ruckus about it, though, she made a mistake common to those who attempt to censor and suppress: She drew attention to the very thing she didn't want people to see.

Face it, "The Last Temptation of Christ" never would have been a box office smash if the Comstock-Christians hadn't tried to keep it out of the theaters. It is unlikely that Cinicinnatians would've lined up around the block to see the Robert Mapplethorpe exhibit if the cops hadn't raided the joint. To go back a few years, James Joyce's "Ulysses"—some of the densest prose on paper—was a best-seller on the basis of its notoriety, not its readability.

Few, if any, of those dirty little sixth-graders would have noticed that ad, and those who did would have given it only a passing, sniggering glance. Now that it has become a focus of controversy, many may have studied it closely and wondered what the 900-number message said.

A few probably become curious enough to dial, then hang up and howl with laughter. The bolder of them might shout an anti-homosexual imprecation into the receiver first. Then, in sixth-grade fashion, they forget all about it until Pop notices that 900 charge on the phone bill, at which point the intrepid callers learn some dandy new swear words, and their corruption is complete.

I'd like to save everyone that unnecessary sorrow and expense by telling exactly what I heard when I dialed that number—no holds barred. First, I heard a screeching tone, then a seductive voice murmured: "We're sorry, your call cannot be completed as dialed. If you feel you have reached this recording in error, please check the number and dial again." I dialed again and got the same message. Not only that, but it was a woman's voice. Man-to-man contact? What a gyp!

And by the way, kids, if you ever need to find the Aral Sea, just go north from India to the 45th parallel. It's the first sea on your left—you can't miss it. And remember, you read it here first.

Even ignorant racists have guarantee of free speech

A UNIVERSITY IS SUPPOSED TO BE A "MARKETPLACE OF IDEAS," WHERE EVERY notion, no matter how extreme, is given full and fair consideration. Some UMC officials apparently are more comfortable with a sort of intellectual convenience store that has a more limited selection.

An idea with admittedly less appeal than a tepid Big Gulp appeared on the campus last week in the form of a flier, headlined, "Attn. UMC Whites!" It invited anyone fitting that description to join "a orginization that was created to protect the white people of America from the 'pro' minority groups threating to destroy our nation."

Full of glaring misspellings, garbled syntax and hand-lettering that looked as though it was done by a left-handed 8-year-old, the flier was distributed on windshields at a campus parking lot last week.

UMC police warned the hate-mongers that by posting the handbills without going through proper channels, they risked a trespassing violation—a moderate, even-handed response.

It wasn't enough, however, for UMC vice chancellor David McIntire, who declared: "Any kind of hate literature, that sort of thing, is deplorable and has no place on this campus." When a reporter asked him whether he would deny the white supremacists the right to free speech, he replied, "Some things, in terms of the whole ethnic civility notion, just are not in good taste and are not acceptable."

I'll agree with him that the flier was both deplorable and tasteless. As for whether such literature should be banned from campus, I couldn't disagree more. Lunatics, too, have a right to free speech at UMC. The U.S. Supreme Court said as much 17 years ago in the case of Barbara Papish vs. the Board of Curators.

Papish, a graduate student, was expelled for handing out a newspaper "containing forms of indecent speech" under the arch of the Memorial Union. The main indecency was on the cover: a cartoon showing policemen raping the Statue of Liberty and the Goddess of Justice.

The university claimed that on campus, freedom of expression should be "subordinated to other interests such as, for example, the conventions of decency in the use and display of language and pictures."

The Supreme Court disagreed, saying that "state colleges and universities are not enclaves immune from the sweep of the First Amendment. ... The mere dissemination of ideas—no matter how offensive to good taste—on a state university campus may not be shut off in the name alone of 'conventions of decency.'"

Do UMC officials need it spelled out any more clearly? If it was unconstitutional to expel Papish for passing out tasteless leftist literature, then an outright ban on right-wing racist handbills would be equally illegal.

No matter how wrong or offensive a political ideology is, it still rates as much space on the campus bulletin boards as advertisements for signet rings or spring break ski trips.

In any case, the controversial flier, with all its blunders and crudity, would hardly be likely to attract any but the most cretinous recruits, and they're already racists. Suppression only drives the ugliness underground, where it can fester and spread and grow like an undiagnosed cancer.

In the open, ridiculous dogmas such as white supremacy can be met head-on and defeated with the weapons of reason and ridicule.

Heterosexuals are source of problems in military

IT'S BECOME COMMONPLACE AMONG COMMENTATORS TO OBSERVE THAT WITH the collapse of the Soviet Union, certain U.S. military chiefs and policymakers have been inconveniently left without a bogeyman to battle.

Consequently, they had to concoct another threat in jig time. Like the big bad Soviet bear, it had to be an apparition so awful and frightening that a majority of Americans could unite in right-thinking opposition.

Finally, a consensus common enemy has emerged: American gays who want the right to serve in the U.S. military.

The public is encouraged to believe the ridiculous canard that the robust character of our armed forces depends largely on the exclusion of openly gay women and men. It's said to be a matter of national security, like the Soviet Union used to be.

The specter most commonly invoked by ignorant people—Congressman Harold Volkmer used it recently—is that of lust-mad male homosexuals attacking red-blooded soaped-up GIs in the barracks showers.

One rather doubts that the Shower scene is a common occurrence in those countries—like Israel, for instance—that allow homosexuals to enlist. But folks like Volkmer and U.S. Sen. Sam Nunn persist in repeating the "Psycho Meets Deliverance" scenario, accompanied by a proper shudder. As if any self-respecting homosexual would give those flabby old men a second glance.

If shower rapes were a problem, of course, the obvious solution would be to make the showers cold. But homosexual misconduct is not a problem in the U.S. military. Hang on to your soap, fellas, the problem is heterosexual misconduct.

The Tailhook incident, described by the cautious New York Times as "a three-day bacchanal" at the Las Vegas Hilton in 1991, was the worst example of flagrant mass sexual misconduct in modern U.S. history. Seven men and 83 women were assaulted, including wives, girlfriends, mothers and sisters of U.S. Navy officers.

Besides the ubiquitous pinching and leering, the sailors and Marines stripped unwilling teenage victims, fondled and bit helpless women and generally dragged the honor of the armed services through the bilge. Nearly three dozen admirals and generals looked on placidly and did nothing to stop them.

The phrase "code of conduct" sounds hollow and cheap in the mouths of such men. Yet they and their ilk are in the forefront of those who demand the exclusion of homosexuals from the ranks.

Want another recent example? An American sailor admitted yesterday that, in a drunken rage, he attacked and killed a homosexual shipmate. The defendant also testified he'd lied when he'd said previously that the shipmate had made homosexual advances.

In fact, the murder happened in a public restroom. The victim hadn't crawled into the sailor's berth or so much as whispered a proposition. He was killed not for anything he did, but for what he was. "I remember hitting him in the face and stomping on his neck and kicking him in the groin," the sailor said.

The U.S. Navy is taking the matter seriously. Airman apprentice Terry Helvey, 21, is charged with premeditated murder. The Navy might actually string this pathetic young gob from the yardarm for killing a gay man.

Perhaps it would take another death to force the Navy to acknowledge the connection between Helvey's blind, homophobic rage and its own official hostility toward homosexuals.

The sailor's bigotry was focused and personal, like that of a lynch mob; the Navy's is institutional and diffuse, like that of country club segregationists. In either guise, it's still bigotry.

Flag desecration debate wears out faint-of-heart

IN MANY RESPECTS, MY LOVE FOR THE UNITED STATES IS AKIN TO A MOTHER'S love for her child—affection and loyalty that is deep and abiding.

"But," as Mom told me on frequent occasions, "I don't always love the things you do." What most makes this country worth loving is the freedom its citizens have to express themselves without government interference, even when their expressions are downright disagreeable—nay, disloyal.

Congress is deliberating yet again whether to make flag desecration a criminal act, this time by means of an amendment to the Constitution. This will be the third try.

It's enough to make a man tired, to make him want to just give up and roll over, like Tribune columnist David Webber did last Monday.

Webber, a longtime opponent of such an amendment, announced on June 23: "I have changed my opinion." His reasoning, insofar as I can follow it, is that the U.S. Supreme Court is making public policy "through its interpretations of constitutional rights," and "these interpretations will increasingly threaten the political system."

An MU associate professor of political science, Webber apparently has far less faith in the strength and resiliency of our political system than I do. Wasn't he around during the '60s? Do the names "Kent State" and "Watts" strike the mystic chord of memory? Talk about threatening the established political order! Still, our system managed to survive without modification to the First Amendment.

As Webber himself said, "Flag desecration is not a big problem." Nevertheless, it apparently calls for a big solution, "more radical than either the proposed term limit or balanced budget amendments," as he wrote.

Of course, it would be no solution at all. A flag-protection amendment would cause more headaches than it would cure. Webber himself noted the "practical problems" with such an amendment: "Can someone burn a huge poster of a flag? What about clothing that bears the image of the flag?" And so forth.

He posed excellent questions and offered no answers. That's probably just as well, because along the way he revealed a certain carelessness with historical fact. "We have never adopted a constitutional amendment to limit citizens' rights and behaviors," he declared.

The infamous 18th amendment, later repealed, aimed to limit citizens' rights and behaviors regarding their consumption of alcoholic beverages. Although a solid majority of citizens backed it when it was passed, Prohibition later turned out to be a bad idea—unenforceable and ultimately counterproductive.

Yet, it is public opinion that seemingly changed Webber's mind. "Polls consistently find that 75 percent of us support a flag-desecration amendment," he pointed out.

An esteemed Tribune editorial writer has already written in response, "It is precisely against this sort of thoughtless bandwagon the Constitution most proudly stands."

Webber longs ungrammatically for a First Amendment "to narrowly protect written and oral expression as a constitutional right" while putting flag desecration and campaign contributions, among other things, on a shorter chain.

But flag burning is a form of political expression. Imagine, for a moment, that the student who stood up to the tanks in Tiananmen Square had also burned a flag—the red flag of the oppressive People's Republic of China. Wouldn't we, watching on television in the United States, have considered that to be political expression? Wouldn't we have cheered his courage and booed when the authorities clapped him in fetters and threw him in prison?

To Webber, the debate boils down to a simple question: "Do we amend the Constitution to protect a valued symbol or further undermine our political system under the guise of protecting free speech?"

Well, when the big whistle blows, I say to hell with the symbol—it's just a symbol—and protect the free speech, in whatever guise it may come. You can't combat "the public's continuing cynicism about our political system" by restricting people's political rights. Might as well try to smother a fire with jellied gasoline.

Besides, you'd think that if Congress were all that concerned about flag burning, it could require all flag manufacturers to use only nonflammable material. But that would be deemed an unreasonable infringement on the manufacturers' right to turn a maximum profit. There are places where even Congress has to draw a line.

'School choice' is no choice for a majority of Americans

A CONTROVERSY LOOMS AS TO WHETHER THE AMERICAN PUBLIC AT LARGE IS ultimately educable, and whether that goal is even worth the effort and expense.

Let me declare myself out front as a fervent believer in public education. Good public schools benefit everyone. There is no more effective crime-fighting tool than public education, no more binding guarantee of future productivity and no better bulwark against a decline in the general prosperity. Also, there is no other way to make democracy work.

Others may disagree with these premises, and often do. Let them get their own columns. They believe the future of American education lies in the private sector. This conviction finds its expression in a debate that rages in Washington, D.C., in Jefferson City and in Columbia about the wisdom of funding private education with public dollars.

Declaring themselves the defenders of "school choice," private schools and their customers are attempting to shoulder themselves a place at the public trough, seeking government subsidization through school vouchers and tuition tax credits for private elementary and secondary education.

This approach poses troubling questions to retro-fitted Jeffersonians like me. To begin with, such a subsidy would be highly regressive. Students in private schools come primarily from upper class or upper-middle-class families. To pay their tuition with public money would line the pockets of the relatively wealthy and disregard those of modest means.

Voucher supporters piously proclaim that their proposals allow poor kids the opportunity to attend swanky private schools. This lame attempt at populist rhetoric is simply so much gas. Vouchers or tuition tax credits would still leave first-rate private education far beyond the wherewithal of most American families. Good public schools are vastly more beneficial to a much broader spectrum of the population.

There is also the outlandish claim that putting tax dollars into private schools would not directly benefit religious organizations. The denial is absurd, considering that thousands of parochial schools could tap into the treasury, expanding their client bases and jacking up their fees.

There is great danger in subsidizing organizations that teach and encourage specific sectarian practices and dogma. It matters not whether the curricula include snake-handling, creationism, jihad, the worship of Odin or contemplation of the Buddha. Putting public money into any such instruction seems to me to be a blatant violation of the First Amendment prohibition against laws that establish religion.

It is also a clear breach of the famous invisible wall that is supposed to separate church and state. Keep in mind that every wall has two sides, and breaches run both ways. If church-run schools start getting public money, some members of the public will start to wonder why churches don't pay taxes.

Many churches have enormous financial holdings, and a lot of those holdings have very little to do with religion. Take a common example: a parking lot. The church might own the lot and lease the spaces, yet it pays neither property tax on the tract nor income tax on the revenue it generates. This custom gives the church a considerable competitive edge over other parking lot owners, landlords, publishing houses, private schools and so forth.

Almost everyone seems pretty comfortable with this arrangement, as long as the churches aren't dipping into the public till. Once churches start receiving tax money, folks might get the idea that those churches ought to be kicking into the kitty just like everybody else.

Advocates of school vouchers and tuition tax credits should ponder long and hard before they put at risk the tax-exempt status of religious organizations. Is it worth slaying that golden goose to concoct what amounts to no more than an omelet?

If parochial schools were to develop a reliance on public funds, it would also invite government interference with their curricula. Suppose, for instance, that the surviving followers of David Koresh were to set up their own school and take advantage of government vouchers to fatten up their thin bottom line. Assume that this school would take pains to inculcate the anti-government values and philosophies laid down by their late prophet.

How would the government respond to the requirement that it nurture this viper in its bosom? And if it moved to squelch the Koreshian Academy on those grounds, what would be the reaction of the typical taxpayer? Inevitably, the federal courts would be called upon to resolve the conundrum, with results that no one could foretell.

The overriding concern about the public bankrolling of private schools, sectarian or otherwise, is that it would ensure a two-tiered system of elementary and secondary education in this country.

Such a system is already prevalent in much of the South, where private schools received a huge impetus from court-mandated integration of public facilities. The whites who could afford it sent their kids to all-white private academies rather than submit to the perceived horrors of school desegregation.

With this exodus came a marked decline in support for public education, especially among property owners, and the public schools got worse. Now, almost every southern parent who can afford it sends his or her kids to private schools—not because those schools have fewer black students but because they have better resources.

Critics of public education like to point out its failures and shortcomings, and they do not lack for examples. Successes also abound, although they are sometimes harder to see.

The country has historically pumped money into some spectacular failures. Witness the war on drugs or the war in Vietnam. But it has yet to make a supreme effort to improve public education.

If we give up that fight, we deserve to lose.

Bad boys wear black, or druggies with buggies

THE INDICTMENT LAST MONTH OF TWO YOUNG AMISH MEN ON DRUG PEDDLING charges stunned the nation—whatever that means in a nation that has become both inured and addicted to shock.

Both suspects are named Abner Stoltzfus, which in Lancaster County, Pa., is like being named John Smith, only more common. They are accused of buying methamphetamine and cocaine from the Pagans, a motorcycle gang, and selling it to other Amish.

There it is. The evil drug nemesis has pervaded the horse 'n' buggy set. The bucolic Pennsylvania countryside, which looks remarkably like it did a century ago, is prey to the same vices as the crumbling inner cities and the affluent suburbs.

The authorities, when they hear bad news, usually cite it as ominous evidence that we need to step up the War on Drugs again, with harsher mandatory prison sentences, more searches and seizures, more snooping, snitching, prying and spying. This blinkered and blindered approach is the reason things have come to this unhappy pass.

The drug prohibitionists are in the position of Hercules, who tried to defeat the Hydra by lopping off its nine heads one by one, only to find that two heads would shoot up from each freshly severed stump. The legendary hero thought up a new strategy, finally winning the day by puffing cigarettes at the monster until, according to studies, it expired in a rank haze of secondary smoke. Or maybe he strangled it. In the words of Bones McCoy, "Dammit, Jim, I'm a medical man, not a classicist!"

What I mean to say is, it seems like every time we enact new measures aimed at decapitating the drug trade, it makes things worse. For every dealer laid low, two more emerge to take advantage of the expanding market. And they emerge in the most unexpected places, to wit: shoofly pie county. How could this happen?

To begin with, the Amish are subject to the same foibles and follies as the rest of humanity, especially that segment of humanity between the ages of 15 and 25.

Realists despite their dress and customs, many Amish communities including those in Lancaster County have institutionalized adolescent misbehavior. They turn a blind eye to a certain amount of drinking, dancing and other carrying on. An Associated Press account termed this practice "timeout." I've also heard it referred to as "wilding."

As described to me, these orgies usually consist of a group gathering in a barn. After inbibing quantities of beer or vile cocktails like vodka and orange soda, the carousers dance to country and western music and maybe smoke a few Marlboros. Afterward, while the older boys and girls hold ad hoc wrassling matches in the haymow, the others race their buggies down deserted moonlit lanes. A few really bad eggs might even go break a window somewhere, or tip over a sleeping cow.

It's not impossible to see how these rustic revels came to include the use of cocaine and methamphetamines. No doubt the proximity of the big city had something to do with it. The teeming metropolises of the Eastern seaboard are easily as depraved as the biblical cities of the Plains. It's hard to remove oneself entirely from worldly matters when you're cheek-by-jowl with Camden, N.J. In any case, Amish kids in Clark, Mo., or Kalona, Iowa, are less likely to scrape up an acquaintance with gangbangers and drug dealers.

But the major factor in the drug infestation is the black market. Drug laws have pushed the prices to the stratosphere, with profits so obscene they would embarrass a manufacturer of athletic footwear.

The current system creates great rivers of cash, and cash always seems to find a corruptible crack in whatever obstacle society decides to erect. If every person has a price—or every 10th person—the illegal drug industry stands prepared to pay it in small unmarked denominations.

Amish are not immune to the power of money. Ask anyone who's ever done business with an Amishman and you'll be told that there's a sharp trader under that flat-brimmed hat. That said, the Amish do tend to take the commandments, including the fifth, far more seriously than your average Rotarian does.

Authorities say the two Abner Stoltzfuses moved about a million dollars worth of meth and coke. Even taking into account the official tendency to inflate such numbers, that's a lot of long green for a couple of 24-year-old hayseeds who never even got a drivers license.

In simpler times, when young Amish reprobates were blowing their minds on booze, at least they didn't have to buy it from motorcycle gangs. They couldn't get rich by selling it to their peers or imprisoned for selling it to federal agents.

The Amish Connection is compelling evidence in the power of the black market to corrupt. It also demonstrates conclusively that the approach we've been using is not working.

PETA rhetoric makes fishing sound exciting

Not since Saint Francis was eaten by worms has anyone displayed more tender affection for animals than the folks at People for the Ethical Treatment of Animals.

As much as they cherish the many-legged, however, animal rights activists just can't seem to get along with most two-legged creatures, poultry excepted. They're always getting into a wrangle with other people, which I guess you're obliged to do if you're going to call yourself an animal rights activist.

Still, they sometimes pick the most unlikely antagonists. After all, who would be a more natural corporate ally of PETA than the makers of Wheaties? But General Mills' decision to put a champion bass fisherman on its box evoked shrieks of protest from PETA. Denny Brauer, a Missouri man, is the latest addition to the pantheon of breakfast champions. His selection brought on some of the most overheated rhetoric heard in many a day.

A PETA letter characterized bass fishing as "tricking small animals into impaling themselves on hooks and ripping them from their homes," and the head of the organization's anti-fishing division described it as "a violent activity."

If I had known fishing was so exciting, I would have gone in for it strong years ago. I always considered it rather serene, sedentary, torpid. … What's the word I'm looking for? I think "boring" about covers it.

Of course, I never had the excitement of actually catching a fish. Perhaps the finny denizens of the deep sensed my raging blood lust beneath the ennui and instinctively avoided my line. I certainly didn't sense it myself.

Brauer pointed out that he and other tournament bass fishermen release their catches alive, but the PETA people believe the catch-and-release practice traumatizes the fish.

Personally, I have to question the assumption that the emotional fragility and home lives of fish can be equated with those of human beings. Pressed, I would say I don't think a fish goes through the seven prescribed stages of grief whenever one of its schoolmates hits the hook and vanishes forever. I doubt it even notices. Unlike some people, however, I can't presume to know what goes on in the mind of a fish.

If the Emotional Mr. Limpet argument is a little wobbly, the claim that fishing isn't a sport rests on even shakier ground. "Anglers have no place next to real sportsmen like Michael Jordan and Tiger Woods," wrote the PETA president. She also believes fishing "requires no athletic skill whatsoever."

It's true that there are a number of pot-bellied professional bass fishermen. Their sport doesn't require the stamina of a long-distance runner, the hair-trigger reflexes of a race car driver or the brute strength of a power lifter. But you know, neither does golf.

Ted Williams, the greatest hitter in the history of baseball, became an expert and avid fly fisherman after his retirement from the diamond. He always claimed that catching a trout demanded better hand-eye coordination than hitting a baseball.

So, where does this PETA person get off flaming Ted Williams, or for that matter, Don Brauer? What does she know about the gladiatorial world of pigskin and horsehide? Even the International Olympic Committee has a difficult time trying to define what constitutes a sport.

Perhaps the PETA folks ought to stick with what they know. Because they do make some powerful arguments. No one can deny they have made significant headway in altering public attitudes and behaviors. For example, you don't see nearly as many people wearing furs as you used to, although truth be told I have never seen very many fur wearers in my social circles. Lots of leather bomber jackets, but very few furs.

There is also a lot less meat eaten than in the olden days, especially red meat. That trend, however, seems to be more a result of health consciousness than of conscience. Similarly, the reaction against large-scale livestock confinement operations stems from a concern for water quality, not from tender feelings toward the hogs.

These obvious facts do little to chill the self-righteous fury of some animal rights activists. Many of them consider the consumption of dairy products to be no less an outrage than the clubbing of baby seals. Now, they're trying to put innocent anglers in the same moral class as Serbian war criminals.

My last word on the gallows will be a denunciation of anyone who wants to outlaw barbecue. For now, I offer them only a well-meant morsel of advice: Pick beans, not fights.

Bush proposes 'partnership' for fox, hens

WHILE HE WOULD NEVER ADMIT IT ON "LARRY KING LIVE," RALPH NADER MUST, in his private moments at the shaving mirror, doubt the wisdom of his campaign that handed the presidency to George W. Bush. The Bush restoration has wrought little but disaster for the environmental causes Nader holds so dear.

At Sequoia National Park last week, the president promised an ominous "new environmentalism for the 21st century," in which business and government would be partners. Where the old environmentalism concentrated on conserving wild and scenic areas, Bush envisions a brave new era of policymaking that will "protect the claims of Mother Nature while also protecting the legal rights of property owners."

It is indeed a whole new definition of environmentalism, one that puts the fox into full partnership with the pullets, in effective charge of their care, feeding and disposition. A White House spokesman gushed fervently about "getting MBAs involved" with environmental policy, and you can bet all those wildlife biologists will be happy to welcome aboard those new colleagues—who will probably be their new bosses.

Bush coupled his new environmental vision with the announcement of nearly $5 billion in funding for our national parks. That includes not a penny for acquisition of new parkland. The entire sum is earmarked exclusively for things like roads, sewer improvements, parking facilities and visitors centers. Worthy projects all, no doubt, but all specifically designed to make the parks more accessible and convenient for the average SUV driver. They have nothing to do with nature.

This proposed partnership seems pretty one-sided to me. I can see how Exxon and Shell could profit from the deal, but what's in it for the Arctic National Wildlife Refuge? In what ways do those silent partners—the snow geese, songbirds, shorebirds and loons—benefit from the Bush administration's idea for oil exploration and development in their habitat? Here's what the U.S. Fish and Wildlife Service Web site said: "Oil development in the Arctic Refuge would result in habitat loss, disturbance and displacement or abandonment of important nesting, feeding, molting and staging areas."

Ah, but such a statement has no place in the new environmentalism. The Bush administration recently excised it from the agency Web site, presumably in the greater interest of the fledgling "partnership." It certainly makes one wonder what exactly the Arctic National Wildlife Refuge is supposed to provide a refuge from.

While seeking to obscure the link between oil development and ecological damage in the Arctic refuge, the administration tries to contrive a connection between the proposed drilling and the energy crisis in California. Bush and vice president Dick Cheney want you to believe that more Alaskan oil would put an end to the rolling blackouts in the Golden State. That's like stocking up on oranges when the apple barrel is running low.

Their other proposed solution for California is to build more nuclear power plants, which the White House likes to describe as a "clean" source of power. It's true that nuke plants don't billow big black clouds of noxious smoke, like coal-burning plants, but Bush and Cheney seem to overlook the fact that nuclear plants produce tons of radioactive waste so toxic we don't even want it shipped through our state on the way to somewhere else. How clean is that? Cheney, for one, seems inclined to blame the Californians for relying too much on conservation.

"Conservation may be a sign of personal virtue," he proclaimed, "but it is not a sufficient basis for a sound comprehensive energy policy." Funny how an administration that puts so much stress on policy through personal virtue—witness the emphasis on "faith-based" charities in lieu of publicly financed welfare—can dismiss it out-of-hand when it concerns energy and the environment.

There is a fundamental conflict between what Bush calls "the claims of Mother Nature" and the demands of capitalist business interests. Either one, left unregulated, will eventually take over everything. Nevertheless, these competing interests can coexist and even complement one another.

Often, the catalyst is government regulation. For example, when government decided in the 1970s to limit how much pollution smokestacks could spew into the air, an entire new industry was created to design, build and sell "scrubbers" that enabled factories to meet the new standards. Although the manufacturers passed on some of those additional costs to consumers, they also passed on considerably less sulfur dioxide.

Today, if the government were to tighten up on gas mileage and automobile emissions standards, the manufacturing sector would pay a lot more attention to designing cleaner-burning, more fuel-efficient vehicles. The same goes for alternative sources of energy. Only 3 percent of the dams in the United States provide hydroelectric power, but there is no incentive to harness this existing resource as long as the petroleum companies can simply sink new oil wells anywhere they want.

A partnership ought to benefit all partners, not just the ones that make campaign contributions.

Watergate showed pitfalls of secrecy

As a few of you might have gathered from a flurry of mentions on television, yesterday marked the 30th anniversary of the Watergate break-in, which inaugurated the most notorious cover-up in the history of the glorious republic and the eventual resignation of President Richard Nixon.

Sadly, three decades is a long time in a country where the typical citizen has the memory not of an elephant but of a goldfish. To many, the Watergate scandal is as obscure as Teapot Dome or Credit Mobilier. It lives on mostly as a suffix—an annoying and lazy tendency of politicians and journalists to attach "-gate" to any scandal that threatens to tar the White House: Monica-gate, Iran-contra-gate, etc.

The anniversary nearly coincides with the recent release of more tape recordings from the Nixon Oval Office. As some readers might remember, Nixon secretly taped all conversations in his office, aiming to edit them later and concoct a historic legacy that would cast him as some kind of latter-day Lincoln. In their raw, unexpurgated form, the tapes make him look more like a cross between Boss Tweed and Mark Fuhrman.

Although it's almost ancient history, the Watergate scandal definitely has its lasting lessons. It ought to remind us that secrecy in government often leads those who govern to act on their worst motives.

Basking in the illusion of privacy, Nixon and those around him often behaved like damn-fool frat boys, trying to one-up each other's ethnic slurs and locker-room anecdotes. Jews, Italians and blacks, among others, were slandered in the most offhand and offensive manner.

Naturally, the president and his minions also tossed around plans to sabotage their political enemies. Some of the president's top aides boasted about how, in their younger days, they'd stuffed the ballot boxes to steal a campus election at the University of Southern California. It was but a short step to lengthy discussions of ways to facilitate burglaries, to use federal agencies such as the IRS to harass political opponents and to eviscerate the Bill of Rights.

If those meetings had been less secret, it's a dollar to a dime that Nixon would not have made the decisions that ultimately brought him down in disgrace.

Now, I am not alleging that President George W. Bush and his aides sit around the Oval Office and bash minorities, swap stories of their sexual conquests or plot felonies. One compelling reason not to allege it is that the current administration is probably not so stupid as to commit such conversations, if they exist, to tape.

Nevertheless, what's known of discussions in the Bush White House could lead a reasonable person to believe that executive sessions there often take on the tone of a Deke house officers' meeting. Witness Bush's private nickname—Pootie-Poot—for Russian President Vladimir Putin. At least Nixon, whatever his faults, liked to read. Bush has never given any indication that he's made it through any book more challenging than "Backcourt Sparkplug."

Whatever it is they talk about, Bush and his boys do seem to have the same penchant for secrecy that characterized the Nixon administration. For example, to keep conversations between Vice President Dick Cheney and energy executives from becoming public, they dredged up the hoary old claim of "executive privilege."

Executive privilege? That's enough to make me assume the discussions centered on ways the executives could despoil the wilderness and screw the consumers. Perhaps there was also some mention of campaign contributions.

The most confidential talks of all, of course, involve the continuing war on terrorism. Bush and his advisers have attempted to frame the issue as one that demands total secrecy, lest Osama bin Laden and his henchmen become wise to our plans to "smoke them out of their holes," to use the president's words. The secrecy also extends to all battlefield operations, civilian casualty counts and the detention and interrogation of suspicious people.

It was in this way, behind closed doors, that the Nixon mob planned and executed covert illegal operations in Chile, Laos and Cambodia. Nixon was first elected in 1968 largely because he bragged of a secret plan to end the war in Vietnam. The war ended, all right, with the last U.S. representatives catching a chopper off the roof of the U.S. Embassy in Saigon and the subsequent communist takeover of all of Vietnam. No wonder Nixon wanted to keep it a secret.

Openness is the oxygen of democratic government. Secrecy is like a powerful medicine. Sometimes it might be necessary in small doses, but too much of it is invariably toxic. That is the lesson of Watergate. It would be a shame to have to learn it all over again the hard way.

Flag pledge becomes meaningless chant

AN UNBELIEVABLE FUROR ERUPTED LAST WEEK ABOUT AN ADDENDUM TO THE Pledge of Allegiance after a federal judge ruled that making schoolchildren recite the words "under God" was an unconstitutional breach of the wall that separates church and state.

The plaintiff, an emergency room physician in California, had sued on the grounds that his young daughter was, for all intents and purposes, forced to utter the phrase even though her family does not acknowledge the existence of the deity.

The plaintiff's daughter is now in hiding because of death threats from the God-loving. The U.S. Senate immediately denounced the decision by a vote of 99-0, and the judge who issued it lost no time in effectively quashing his own ruling.

Now, I love a good dust-up as much as anyone—more, in fact. This one, however, is at bottom meaningless. The decision applied only to a portion of the country, and it is bound to be overturned anyway.

More to the point, the pledge itself holds little meaning for the millions of schoolchildren who recite it dutifully each day. The Pledge of Allegiance is a rote exercise. Kids are drilled in it as soon as they are old enough to chew their food, and they perform both tasks with an equal amount of thought and reverence.

A parent I know tells me his 3-year-old daughter has the pledge memorized, but only phonetically. "It means about as much to her as 'eeny-meeny-miney-moe' and a lot less than 'twinkle, twinkle, little star,' " he said.

As an experiment, I posed a question to three 12-year-old boys: What is the meaning of the word, "indivisible?" The answers were: 1. Something that can't be divided; 2. Something that can't be seen; 3. Something in the national anthem.

I didn't ask them to define "under God," or "liberty" or "justice." Those are words that even distinguished federal jurists often struggle with, not to mention the rest of us patriotic citizens.

The pledge was penned in 1892, and the nettlesome "under God" phrase was added in 1954 at the behest of the Knights of Columbus, presumably to differentiate us from the godless communism we were fighting in those days.

Now, the Knights of Columbus is a fine organization, and they really know how to run a bingo hall. But they aren't exactly the Continental Congress, either.

Nevertheless, there is a furious debate about whether the United States was or was not founded as a theistic nation. The political consensus seems to be that our nation's founders were devout believers to a man, that they considered this to be a Christian nation but wisely provided that the law not promote any particular sect. Did not Thomas Jefferson write, in the document we celebrate this week, of a "Creator" who endowed humankind with certain inalienable rights?

No doubt the founders were predominantly Christian, and strictly Protestant Christians, for the most part. They erected that famous wall of separation primarily to prevent the Catholic-Protestant quarrels that had plagued Europe for centuries, and still do, in places.

But I think they had a larger idea in mind: In this country you can say anything you want to say, and no one can make you say anything you don't want to say.

That and that alone is what makes the United States unique among nations.

Surveys show that about 8 percent of the U.S. population is non-believing, a figure that fluctuates according to natural disasters, the jobless rate and other factors. The atheistic element probably was proportionately smaller in 1776 than it is now, but a few freethinkers like Ben Franklin were lurking about even then. Tom Paine, author of "The Rights of Man," was a secular humanist 200 years before that unfortunate term was coined. I can't believe that Jefferson would have denied them the right to hold their damnably dangerous opinions.

That is what freedom is all about. Freedom has nothing to do with flags and fireworks, which are found in every dictatorship in the world.

Celebrate Independence Day. Say whatever you want to.

ACLU: Not just for liberals anymore

WE IN FREEDOM'S LAND AND BRAVERY'S HOME OWE A DEBT OF GRATITUDE TO THE No. 1 enemy of political correctness in our nation—and I sure don't mean Rush Limbaugh.

I refer to the American Civil Liberties Union, long considered by many mainstream conservatives to be the Great Satan of U.S. politics. The ACLU fights against the establishment of organized prayer in government schools. It works to overturn the death penalty and to protect the rights of criminal suspects, even those with names such as Mohammed. It is a friend to flag-burners and a tireless advocate of abortion rights.

No wonder the organization is anathema to so many rightward-leaning Americans. And yet, it is not uncommon to read sentences such as the following, from a weekend Associated Press story: "TIPS was part of President George W. Bush's recently released homeland security plan, but it drew fire from Republican conservatives and from the ACLU, which charged that it would encourage 'government-sanctioned Peeping Toms.' "

Technically, TIPS stands for Terrorism Information and Prevention System, but that's really a mouthful, so you can just think: Tattlers, Informers, Priers and Snoops.

The GOP-controlled House of Representatives wrote TIPS out of the homeland security bill it passed last Friday, and the vote must have been a blow to U.S. Attorney General John Ashcroft, who basically thought up the program and sought to put it into practice almost immediately.

Ashcroft described TIPS as "a clearinghouse for people who think they see something" and not, the AP said, "an Orwellian database that could be used against innocent citizens."

That's a distinction that could lead to a lot of tricky questions and the overuse of quote marks. For instance, what is the difference between a "clearinghouse" and a "database"? What do you mean by "see something"? And who among us is entirely "innocent"? Besides me, I mean.

The attorney general hastened to assure the congressmen that TIPS was not "a program related to private places like homes," but he also tried—unsuccessfully—to recruit U.S. Postal Service carriers to participate. His plan would have enlisted millions of utility workers, train conductors, ships mates and truckers—anyone "seeing things happen that don't usually happen."

"Things that don't usually happen" is a pretty broad brush, one that covers everything from a hole in one to a federal budget surplus and a whole lot in between. It pretty much leaves it up to the individual baggage handler or meter reader to decide which activities are suspicious enough to be reported to the government. It sounds to me like Ashcroft wanted to transform us into East Germany, only with churches and decent restaurants.

I believe he has too little faith in the American people. In the nearly 11 months since the terrorist attacks, they have been duly sensitized to be on the alert for suspicious activity. They don't need to be signed up as officially designated government spies.

Most truck drivers display Old Glory prominently on their rigs, and they will not hesitate to report it if they think someone could be hauling a dirty bomb to a major metropolitan center. Mail carriers, who are themselves at risk from letter bombs, anthrax and other terrorist threats, are unlikely to overlook any dubious and irregular packages they have to deliver.

Congressional Republicans are to be commended for opposing Ashcroft's plan. It was a rare display of true conservative principles. At the risk of contracting liberal cooties, they joined with Democrats such as Sen. Pat Leahy and the ACLU to keep the police state at bay—at least for the moment.

Politicians of both parties can claim nonpartisan motives, but none can do so as convincingly as the ACLU. It's an organization that promotes freedom for all of us—even the bigots and blasphemers. There's nothing more nonpartisan than that.

Defend marriage one couple at a time

IT'S HIGH TIME SOMEONE CAME TO THE DEFENSE OF MARRIAGE. HEAVEN KNOWS the institution has been taking some pretty hard hits for a pretty long time.

Gay marriage—based on the ridiculous notion that homosexual people can actually fall in love—is only the latest in a long series of assaults on marriage.

It's hard to pinpoint just where it started, but liberal wisenheimers were knocking marriage as far back as about 400 B.C.

"By all means, marry," Socrates said. "If you choose wisely, you shall be happy. If you choose badly, you shall become a philosopher."

Serious attacks on marriage go back at least as far as England's Henry VIII, the messiness of whose divorces took on historic dimensions. The institution has steadily eroded ever since, largely as a result of women coming to be recognized in most countries as something more than their husbands' chattels.

Until relatively recently, however, a powerful stigma clung to divorce. It was a political axiom, for example, that no divorced man could ever hope to be elected president of the United States—until one finally was in the person of Ronald Reagan.

The latest figures for U.S. marriages indicate that 55 percent of them are unsuccessful, meaning they end in divorce. Only 45 percent are deemed successful, which I guess means they end in widowhood.

The statistic does not reflect the state of marriages in which the partners co-exist miserably until death mercifully intervenes. It's also skewed by those people who marry two, three four or more times.

I'm confused about how to classify the latter group. Are they attackers or defenders of marriage? Obviously they have unquenchable faith in the institution, and they're very good for the wedding industry—a multibillion-dollar-a-year business. But do multiple marriages indicate a reverence for marriage or disregard for wedding vows?

How much does Madonna revere marriage? What about Liz Taylor, Dennis Rodman and Britney Spears? Some of these knuckleheads put the same level of commitment into holy matrimony that you or I would put into a blind date. For them, it's a way to spend an evening.

So, it makes me squeamish when people say they want to defend marriage with a constitutional amendment defining marriage as something solely between a man and a woman. One might understand if they claimed to be protecting the overburdened Social Security system from a potential flood of new recipients. But I can't see how codifying the predominant gender equation would lend a significant boost to marriage itself.

Although I don't have the figures in front of me, I'll take a wild stab and guess that something like 99.999 percent of the problems in American marriages stem from conflict between men and women. It's hard to imagine how the inclusion of homosexuals could add significantly to the indignities visited on the state of wedlock.

Leaving aside practical factors such as property, pregnancy and hospital visitation, what is the spiritual motivation behind the decision to marry? It's the desire to stand up in front of the whole world—"Before God and these witnesses"—and say: "This is the one!"

In most places, it's still frowned upon to make that statement about a person of the same sex. It can get you beheaded or merely beaten up. For gay people to take their public vows requires a firmer resolve than that it does for straight couples.

It would take a long-term study to determine whether gay marriages have the same staying power as the conventional kind. My guess is they would be about the same, but there wouldn't be so many kids affected by the divorces.

Millions of Americans deplore homosexuality as an abomination and gay marriage as an exponential abomination—and that is their right. Their churches, if churchgoers they be, may refuse to recognize the sanctity of such unions. That is not a matter for government.

Government may make some rules, like limiting each person to one spouse at a time or enacting age minimums or writing the tax code to favor married couples over single people.

But whom to marry is the most personal of decisions. If "the pursuit of happiness" is an inalienable right, surely that right ought to extend to each person's choice of husband or wife.

The U.S. Supreme Court said as much in 1967, when it threw out a Virginia law that forbade interracial marriages. It was not a popular decision at the time, but today only a few unreconstructed bigots would question it as a matter of law or moral rightness.

If you want to defend marriage, defend your own. Make it an exemplar of a loving, devoted partnership—whether you're straight or gay. That shouldn't require a constitutional amendment.

And if it does, you're well on your way to becoming a Socratic philosopher.

Let's shut down the abortion clinics

EVER SINCE I GAVE UP BEATING MY SPOON ON THE HIGH CHAIR AND TOOK UP column writing as a mode of expression, I have always stated that matters of reproductive choice should be strictly between a woman and her physician.

Recent circumstances have obliged me to alter that view. I now believe such matters should be limited to a brief commercial transaction between the woman and the Walgreen's clerk.

In great news for abortion doctors, however, Food and Drug Administration acting Director Steven Galson last week refused to allow over-the-counter sale of Plan B, a morning-after pill produced by Barr Pharmaceuticals. He did so against the recommendations of two advisory panels and the agency's own staff.

Plan B, taken within 72 hours of fertilization, reliably terminates an unwanted pregnancy at its earliest stages. It has no side effects, creates no "high" and is reported to be safer than Tylenol. It could effectively put abortionists out of business.

You'd think such a breakthrough would occasion general rejoicing on all sides of the abortion issue. Women would have a safe and noninvasive way to end unwanted pregnancies. Abortion opponents could breathe a sigh of relief because those adorable, thumb-sucking fetuses featured on the roadside billboards would no longer be slaughtered by the thousands.

Such details matter not to many Americans, including those who currently run the country. They purport to believe that the quality of personhood coincides with the instant of conception. When a gamete meets a gamete, there appears in a twinkling an incipient individual with all the protections and dignities due any taxpaying, civic-minded, lodge-joining member of society. The rights of the microscopic blastula are thought to outweigh those of the lung-breathing, soul-searching woman in whose body it resides.

Many, many of these cell clusters are lost in naturally occurring early miscarriages, which the woman often experiences as nothing more than a heavy menstrual flow. No one mourns. Such things are, after all, a part of God's plan. If the plan called for a case of sudden infant death syndrome, however, deep grieving would be not just appropriate but unavoidable.

That's because a baby and a zygote really are different. Every human feels this instinctively.

Nancy Reagan certainly recognizes the distinction, which is why she could come out last week in public support of fetal stem-cell research. This field of study offers great promise in fighting diseases such as Parkinson's, diabetes and Alzheimer's that attack real people like Ronald Reagan, Christopher Reeves, Muhammad Ali and millions of lesser celebrities.

At least a dozen Republican U.S. senators, some of them staunchly anti-abortion, also take what I would call a pro-real-life position on this groundbreaking medical research. They console themselves with the knowledge that the fetuses used in such studies would have been destroyed anyway as part of the standard procedure.

It should be noted that acting FDA Director Galson did not specifically mention fetal rights in his rejection of Plan B's over-the-counter availability. His stated concerns are for girls younger than 16 who might use the emergency contraception in lieu of condoms, making these young girls more vulnerable to sexually transmitted diseases. So, they should definitely be required to see a doctor, right?

That reasoning fails to address the needs of the 98 percent of sexually active women older than 15, however, and it also ignores the fact that Plan B has to be taken within 72 hours to be effective.

Try making an ob-gyn appointment on three days' notice. It'll be more like three weeks, if you're lucky, and it doesn't matter how old you are—only how rich. I guess Galson never thought about that, having never in his life been required to schedule an ob-gyn appointment. Now, why would that be? Oh, that's right, because he's a man.

This third-tier male bureaucrat has made a historic decision, because this technology could be truly revolutionary.

A safe and effective morning-after pill, universally available, would make surgical abortion practically obsolete. The disappearance of this gruesome and invasive procedure might ultimately bring an end to the wrenching debate that divides people of good will. Would this not be a great thing for our country? Ah, but there could be even larger issues at work here.

Consider: Why are so many men opposed to the idea of a morning-after pill? What would they have to lose? It isn't as though men everywhere are lining up to put on condoms or pay child support on their bastards.

Let's be clear. This issue is about men controlling women, who still have to negotiate a daunting series of manmade obstacles to exercise any control over their reproductive choices. The object is, as it has always been, to make sure promiscuous women pay dearly for their pleasures. It goes back to Eve, who unwisely let herself be seduced by the serpent and then induced Adam to make it a three-way.

Thus was paradise lost, and women have been taking the blame ever since. Believe it if you want, but it's a poor basis for public policy.

Public defenders chronically under-funded

THE MISSOURI STATE AUDITOR RECENTLY FAULTED THE STATE PUBLIC DEFENDER'S office for improper spending of the taxpayers' money, which is like blaming baby seals for the emission of carbon dioxide gases: Yes, technically they do it, but it's a tiny amount, and besides, they really can't help it.

At issue is the public defender's occasional representation of clients who are not legally indigent as defined by statute. The audit found that the practice amounts to a misuse of state resources.

The defender's office acknowledges that not everyone it represents is flat broke. But hey, public defenders don't get to select their own clientele. If they did, they'd get a lot more favorable verdicts because the fact is that almost everyone unfortunate enough to end up as part of the public defender's caseload is not only poor but also guilty.

Guilty or innocent, every criminal defendant does have the right to a competent attorney, albeit an overworked and underpaid one. The U.S. Supreme Court decreed as much more than 40 years ago.

When a defendant pleads poverty, the judge assigns his or her case to a public defender. Trouble is, some of these defendants exceed the laughably low income standard below which free legal assistance is supposed to kick in.

Should the public defender refuse to take the case, he or she risks a contempt citation that could mean jail time—not to mention the lasting enmity of the circuit judge. The Missouri Supreme Court has ruled judges have the right to assign cases to the public defender even when the client is ineligible.

The eligibility standard in Missouri is set at the federal poverty line, which means a single person working full time for minimum wage does not qualify. That's a little more than $10,000 annually, as Tribune reader Ruth O'Neill pointed out in an Open Column letter that ran Sunday. She also noted that ownership of a car worth more than $2,000 or the ability to borrow $5,000 for bail money are also grounds for disqualification. And the going rate for the services of a private attorney is rarely less than $100 per hour.

A lot of people who make more than the minimum wage still have to struggle to make it to the next paycheck. The hard reality is that many low-wage workers couldn't afford a private attorney if their lives depended on it—and sometimes their lives do depend on it.

Judges are aware of these factors, and they also know that if a defendant is tried and convicted without a proper lawyer, the conviction is likely to be overturned on appeal. That means a retrial and a real waste of public resources, so the magistrates tend to err on the side of caution.

There is a provision in the law that requires recipients to fill out eligibility forms, and there exists a procedure that allows the defender's officer to bill a client who turns out to be ineligible for public legal assistance.

But let's return to the real world again, shall we? To generalize, most accused criminals whose cases wind up in the public defender's office are the sort of people who tend to have trouble with paperwork and the timely paying of bills.

The state audit found that when the public defenders billed their not-quite-indigent clients, the collections averaged out to $16 per case. You can squeeze those turnips as hard as you want and not get enough blood to make a meal for a mosquito.

It's unfair to blame the public defenders, the circuit judges or even the auditor's office whose investigation has served to cast a light on the inadequacy of the system.

Inadequate, yes, but it's not really wasteful in the larger scheme of things. There is so much appalling waste in government spending. You can read about it every day. Think of the millions in relief aid sent to Florida hurricane victims who, it turns out, weren't actually victimized. The Pentagon lays out enough money to hire Johnny Cochran, and all it gets are a few toilet seats. The mayor of Columbia wants to spend $60,000 in transportation grant money to gussy up a couple of city buses so they'll look like trolley cars.

Sixty thousand, you say? That's probably enough right there to cover a public defender's annual salary, with enough left over for a paralegal.

Yep, government spending is pretty wasteful, but less so if the money is to be spent on poor people. Then, government tends to get frugal—except when it comes to prison construction, i.e., high-cost public housing for young black men. Most politicians are loath to spend money on people who don't already have it.

The current thinking seems to be: Let's give rich people more money to create more incentive for poor people to be rich. They'll work harder that way, you see.

You can agree or disagree with that analysis. The fact is there is no constitutional right to government cheese, Head Start classes, lifesaving surgery or any other facet of the much despised "nanny state."

But there is in this great country the constitutional right to an attorney for every criminal defendant, even a poor one. It is one of our bulwarks against the awesome prosecutorial power of the government. It is one of our freedoms.

And as the tight-lipped neoconservatives never tire of telling us: Freedom isn't free.

Smoking ban smacks of Puritanism

Sticking up for unpopular causes and people has always been something of a specialty of mine. Holocaust deniers, gay bridegrooms, death row inmates, progressive taxers, drug law reformers, race-baiters and abortionists: These I have defended with all the arguments at my disposal.

But defending tobacco smokers? That's edging mighty close to beyond the pale. With the possible exception of unrepentant pederasts, no group is more universally condemned by all right-thinking, upstanding Americans than the pathetic puffer of cigarettes.

His teeth stained a stunning shade of teak, with the breath of a cannibal and a foul stink pervading his hair and clothing, the smoker is rebuked and scorned by one and all. He is shunned by polite company, and even small children do not hesitate to call him out for his vile and disgusting practice.

So it is with some trepidation that I or anyone can openly oppose the proposal to ban tobacco entirely from Columbia's bars and restaurants. For me, it's also a case of special pleading, for I belong to the class of miserable wretches that smokes cigarettes.

People ask: Why don't you just quit? I have made several serious attempts, and the end result has been job loss and personal alienation. Abandoning my usual serenity, I was transformed into a great two-legged bundle of irritable tics and irrational outbursts, exacerbated by splinters in my tongue from chewing toothpicks.

But let's leave my personal shortcomings aside—please!—and talk instead about the ordinance, which would prohibit smoking altogether in bars, bowling alleys and bingo halls as well as eateries, where it is now restricted but sometimes allowed.

The most compelling argument for the ban is that secondhand smoke constitutes a health hazard and nonsmokers should not be involuntarily put at risk.

Some researchers who do not have a political agenda claim the science touting the risks of secondhand smoke is dubious. I don't doubt for a moment that secondhand smoke is bad for you, just as SUV exhaust, red meat, rye whiskey and elevator music are bad for you.

But I do believe anti-smoking zealots do not hesitate to overstate the real risks to someone who occasionally or even frequently visits a smoking venue. Dueling studies are bound to be featured during the upcoming debate.

We firsthand smokers, on the other hand, know all too well the price we eventually might have to pay. Our hawking and hacking are the harbingers of the far worse consequences to come. We also know the social costs of smoking: the snubs, the curled lips and hostile glares. We retreat to the parking lot or the loading dock during the sub-freezing midwinter days, standing uncovered in the sleet just to satisfy our nasty addiction. Talk about a health risk!

Certainly, there ought to be places for nonsmokers to go where they don't have to inhale tobacco smoke, where they don't go home red-eyed and reeking of cigarettes. As a matter of fact, there are already dozens of such places in Columbia alone, where diners and tipplers can enjoy themselves in a fume-free atmosphere.

At the same time, there also ought to be places for those of us who know the risks of smoking and choose to assume them are still welcome to spend our money and drink a cold beer, for cryin' out loud.

This is where the free market is supposed to kick in. People who abhor smoking are free to steer clear of the bars and restaurants where it is allowed. Restaurant and bar owners should be free to choose their own policies regarding smoking, based on what brings in the most business—or keeps the least business away.

If the ordinance does pass, I hope some open-minded entrepreneur will establish a private nightclub where patrons can pay a membership fee and, once they cross the threshold, are allowed to dissipate in any legal manner they want to—even if that means lighting up.

We love to talk about "freedom" in this country, to the point that the term begins to lose all meaning. Maybe it has already, if it no longer covers the right of every American to go to hell by the route of his or her own choice.

Did you hear they've banned smoking in Cuba? That ought to tell you something.

Casting a cryptic eye on Christ, Forrest visits the sepulcher at Our Lady of Sorrows Shrine in Starkenburg, Mo., in 1999.

CHAPTER 2

RELIGIOUS PURSUITS

Attacks on Halloween scarier than the holiday

Not to unduly alarm anyone, but there's an especially creepy specter abroad in the land this Halloween season. Roving bands of peevish grown-ups armed with personal agendas are putting the kibosh on Halloween finery.

The religious right and the commissars of political correctness—as gruesome a pair of bedfellows as you'd ever dread to meet—are crusading for Halloween costume reform in my old stumbling grounds of southeast Iowa, according to an article last week in the Cedar Rapids Gazette.

A certain Rev. Tuttle in Marion, Iowa, summed up one point of view. Instead of masquerading as witches, ghosts and goblins, he said, Halloween celebrants should "change back to a Christian holiday" and dress up as biblical characters.

He expressed the view that scary costumes amount to devil worship and said: "Last week, I asked kids if they see any satanic signs around schools and neighborhoods. Several hands went up." The Rev. Tuttle went on to denounce "this haunted house experience—going through dark places and being scared. Who needs that?"

Personally, I'm with pastor Tuttle on the haunted house thing. Why pay money to have a guy in a ski mask pretend to attack you with a chain-saw in a darkened hallway?

On the other hand, what appeals to the Rev. Tuttle and me is irrelevant. There is a vast number of preadolescents and other people out there who dearly love the quiver of goose flesh and the delicious sensation of pumping adrenalin. Let them have it, I say.

As for his claim that Halloween was originally a Christian holiday, most of the holiday's traditions were Druidical, with a few, like bobbing for apples, borrowed from the Roman harvest festivals. The early Christians employed a shrewd strategy of encouraging converts by coopting pagan festivals and holidays. Thus was Halloween grafted onto the Christian calender as All Saints Eve.

Tuttle's Halloween-as-satanism angle, embraced largely by fundamentalists, bears close scrutiny. Perhaps, as the young churchgoers' testimony implies, there really is a widespread devil-worship movement in Marion. Before leaping to that conclusion, though, consider the unfortunate episodes in Salem, Mass., where child witnesses were so imaginative and eager to please that innocent women were burned as witches.

When public schools have Halloween parties, parents frequently protest on the grounds that such functions amount to school support for witchcraft and devil worship, said an attorney for the Iowa Department of Education. Accordingly, many districts discourage students from dressing up as witches, skeletons, demons or ghosts.

No witches or ghosts on Halloween? It might make a certain kind of sense to crusade for the removal of Santa Claus and the Easter Bunny so that

Christians may focus more intently on the spiritual implications of their most holy days. But they have no business dictating in the matter of Halloween costumes. It's not their area.

For all their self-righteous fomenting, however, the fundamentalists are making much the same point as the people who claim the U.S. Constitution prohibits Christmas pageants. I can entertain the church/state argument a good deal more sympathetically than I can that of the Iowa City school district's Equity Affirmative Action Advisory Committee—EAAAC to its friends.

The committee recommended that "teachers and parents be sensitive to costumes that could be hurtful or portray others in a negative way." The district's equity coordinator—that's really her title—said such costumes include "those portraying gypsies, American Indians, old people and hoboes."

It takes a bunch of serious-minded adults in committee form to reach a conclusion like that one. It would never occur to the kids.

The little girl who transforms herself with colorful sateen dress, scarf and sash isn't being disrespectful to gypsies; she's romanticizing gypsies. The same goes for the depictions of American Indian chiefs and princesses. Little boys who dress as hoboes aren't taunting homeless people; they're imagining the charms of life on the open road, living on handouts. And young people masquerading as old people is not nearly as offensive as some of the things crones and geezers do in order to appear younger than they are.

Observing the two-front assault on Halloween traditions, one poet-philosopher I know forecast a grim, Orwellian future in which the only allowable costume would be Barney, the unspeakable purple TV dinosaur. Halloween nights, he said, will be overrun by armies of Barneys.

Now, *that's* scary.

Christians can't complain about treatment in America

Do you hear that whining noise like a buzz saw through reinforced concrete? Annoying, isn't it? It's the sound of Ralph Reid and the other Christian Coalitionists complaining they're being picked on by government and the media.

Whenever I hear this noise, I stop whatever I'm doing, seal my ears with paraffin and thumb through Thieleman van Braght's "Martyrs Mirror." Nothing restores the old perspective like the accounts of real persecution and real sufferings endured by real ...

Oops, I almost said real Christians! And that would be implying the coalitionists aren't as truly Christian as the 16th century Anabaptists were. Heaven forfend! No, my only point is that when these modern-day churchmen claim to be the victims of official maltreatment or media neglect, they are talking through their hats.

The best proof is a quick scan of your radio dial. Wherever you are, you're bound to pull in at least one or two Christian stations over the public airwaves. Such stations often outnumber all the rest, and in certain parts of the South on Sundays you'll find the entire spectrum given over completely to preaching and religious music. Heard any Islamic radio shows lately?

Christian television ministries are nearly as ubiquitous as radio and, for the churches, far more profitable. Regular commercial broadcasters dedicate much air time to devotional programming of the Christian variety, not to mention granting generous news coverage to the works of local churches and the Christian religion in general.

The lavish coverage of Pope John Paul II's recent visit to the United States would lead one to believe the Messiah himself was on hand and not just his earthly representative. Day after day, it was the lead story. Even the government-run-liberal-elitist National Public Radio treated Il Papa's tour as an event of historic importance. It wasn't.

Oh, I have no objection to NPR or any other media outlet playing the story big. I bring it up merely to illustrate how ludicrous is the notion that Christians as a group are maligned or ignored by the news media. They aren't.

As for government, I haven't really noticed a marked anti-Christian tendency. Most politicians pander shamelessly to Christian churchgoers, and even those who don't are careful to mouth the standard pieties.

Pieties like that engraved on our coinage: "In God We Trust." Then, there's the adverbial phrase "under God," which was inserted into the Pledge of Allegiance by President Dwight D. Eisenhower. Does anyone doubt the deity referred to is the god of Abraham?

It beats me why the coalition churchmen should be so down on government. In substantial ways, the predominant religions in this country—that is, the prosperous ones—benefit mightily from government munificence. Public money builds the roads that lead to their fine churches—and to the church parking lots they rent out on football Saturdays. Public money pays for their fire and police protection, not to mention keeping many parishioners financially afloat. Considering churches pay no taxes, they've got a pretty good deal.

Still, there are those who insist the Christian religion should swing greater weight in public policy, particularly in the schools.

My wife and I this month attended a meeting of parents with the principal of the Columbia public school our son attends. During the general discussion, a parent addressed the principal: He was Jewish, he said, and he wanted to know whether the school was going to emphasize Christmas again this year.

Christmas stuff is everywhere you go, he reminded us: stores, streets, restaurants, malls. He's finding it tough to keep his children focused on the faith of their fathers, he said, concluding: "I just think the public schools is the one place they shouldn't have all that pushed on them." A dark man rumbled his heavily accented agreement: Religion is a private family matter, he said. Not for schools. His veiled wife nodded silently.

Their frustration was obvious and understandable. Christianity is very nearly the official religion of this country, and other faiths are perceived as alien and unwelcome, especially in politics.

Christians ought to be the last to complain.

Ask Falwell: What would Jesus do?

MILLIONS OF PEOPLE BELIEVE GOD SPEAKS THROUGH THE REV. JERRY FALWELL, and it is certainly true that his voice is heard worldwide. With a few ill-chosen words last week, he managed to spark riots in India that left nine people dead and scores more injured.

On the television program "60 Minutes," Falwell offered his opinion that the prophet Mohammed, founder of Islam, was not a holy man but instead "a terrorist." Some of India's Hindus apparently agreed, and they clashed with some of their Muslim countrymen.

India's warring sects don't need much of an excuse to get after one another. It was difficult to fathom why a just and merciful God—speaking through a paunchy, prosperous and highly political Virginia soul-salver—would apply a match to such dry tinder.

Subsequently, Falwell said his remarks were "a mistake," which I guess rules out the possibility that they were divinely inspired. But it took criticism from the secular authorities in Great Britain and other countries to make him see the light at last.

Falwell said he reached his controversial conclusion after a careful study of the Quran, the Muslim holy book. He said it showed him that Mohammed was "a violent man—a man of war," in stark contrast to the peaceful dispositions of Judeo-Christian icons Moses and Jesus.

Muslims, naturally, were incensed at what they perceived as a slur on their faith and its leading prophet. Grand Ayatollah Mohammed Hussein Fadlallah warned the faithful not to resort to physical violence against the infidel Falwell, no matter how misguided his views. Islam, the ayatollah declared, "is a religion of mercy and love."

Almost all organized religions make the same claim, and almost every one of them has also felt obliged, at some point in its history, to engage in slaughter and persecution to reinforce the rightness of its dogma.

Regrettably, my knowledge of Islam and its founding prophet is pretty scanty. Unlike Falwell, I don't pretend to be any sort of authority. Nor am I an expert on the Bible. I have read enough of it, though, to know that a good many Old Testament prophets were no peaceniks. Many of them were in fact quite ready to resort to violence.

The jawbone-wielding Samson slew a thousand men. The warrior Joshua, having brought down the walls of Jericho with shouts and trumpets, "utterly destroyed all that was in the city, both man and woman, young and old, and ox and sheep and ass with the edge of the sword." Even gentle Balaam beat his jackass in a manner that would appall the ASPCA. The list is long.

Jehovah himself, in those rough and ready days, did not hesitate to smite individual sinners, rain fire on wicked cities or even flood the entire Earth when the mood was upon him. In Moses' time, Jehovah visited a series of plagues upon the Egyptian slavemasters and ended up killing all of their firstborn sons.

This was the same God that Falwell claimed last year had allowed the attacks of Sept. 11 to occur because of New York City's overall depravity—especially its tolerance of homosexuality.

Jesus introduced a whole new way of thinking. In the first century A.D., "Love thy neighbor as thyself" and "Turn the other cheek" were novel, even revolutionary, concepts.

Christ, however, was not uniformly lamblike. In his most famous display of temper, Jesus erupted in the Great Temple of Jerusalem, overturning the tables of the moneychangers and driving them from that sacred place. It is a scriptural passage that should strike fear into the hearts of money-grubbing televangelists—unless, that is, in their hearts they don't really believe it.

For all its unintended consequences, Falwell's thoughtless blurting has raised a crucial question, one that many Christians consider central to their belief system: What would Jesus do?

It's a good question, when one considers the current crisis in the Middle East, but it's not an especially difficult question. He would no doubt deplore the brutal regime of Saddam Hussein. There's no reason to believe he wouldn't be equally disapproving of Israel's harsh occupation of the West Bank or the heavy-handed oppression practiced by the rulers of Saudi Arabia. For that matter, he probably wouldn't smile on the greed and corruption of Western capitalism, either.

The question at hand, however, is how he would react to the determination of the U.S. government to launch a military invasion of Iraq. Would he assume that airstrikes alone would do the job, or would he insist on the necessity of ground forces? I wonder precisely what level of civilian casualties he would consider acceptable.

You don't have to have a doctorate in theology to make a pretty persuasive argument that Jesus would have been less than satisfied with any of the aforementioned courses of action. I'll go way out on a limb and say he would have supported further negotiation that would lead to disarmament—preferably universal disarmament. But he'd probably agree to start with Saddam's Iraq.

OK, it might be too late to beat our smart bombs into smart plowshares. At the same time, our leaders both religious and secular should be careful about invoking the name of Jesus Christ to justify what will surely be an extremely bloody and violent affair.

For who can know the mind of God? No mortal man can, and certainly not a recalcitrant sinner like me. But the Rev. Jerry Falwell, for all his impressive credentials and unshakeable confidence, possesses all the spiritual insight of a shock jock and somewhat less than that of a squeegee man.

He's living proof that you can't judge the nature of a modern religion by the character of its founding prophets.

'Design' law debases science and religion

UNTIL THE DAY I FINALLY DIP MY TOE IN THE BRIMSTONE, I SHALL ALWAYS BE grateful to Mrs. Weed. She didn't teach a whole lot of advanced biology to our third-grade class—we were still trying to differentiate the pistil and stamen. One day, though, the history of the human species came up for discussion.

At the time, I was enthralled by the Time/Life book on evolution, with its famous ape-to-man stepladder illustration. I warmed to the subject, only to encounter intense ridicule from my classmates. One mean girl—Linda was her name—got right in my face and jeered: "Your grandpa is a monkey!" I secretly suspected she might be right but nevertheless responded hotly.

Then Mrs. Weed interjected: "Many scientists believe as Forrest does."

Actually, because this was Dallas, Texas, what she said was: "Many sahntists believe as Farst does." Thank you, Mrs. Weed. So there, Linda!

Evolution was an article of faith in our house. So was God—and Jesus, too. That never struck me as a contradiction at the time, and even now I don't see the concepts as irreconcilable. Perhaps that's because in our family, we weren't taught to read the Bible literally. Oh, we had plenty of Bible lessons, but we knew, for instance, that "to walk a mile in the shoes of another" did not involve an actual exchange of footwear.

Our reading of the Old Testament was even looser. The stories of Adam and Eve's expulsion from Eden or Noah and the flood we assumed to be straightforward tales with the moral: If you're bad, you'll be punished. And isn't that really the point? The Bible is about right and wrong. It was never intended to be a science textbook. It doesn't have to be reconciled with science any more than "Huckleberry Finn" or the "Hallelujah Chorus" must be reconciled with science.

The Missouri General Assembly is about to require the state's biology teachers to instruct their students in the concept of "intelligent design" as an alternative to evolution.

ID, as it is called, sees the whole universe—from the vast tracts of empty space to the single-celled protozoa to the modern-day professional wrestling fan—as something that was planned and executed by …

Well, by something. The nature of the designer is left purposefully vague to evade potential constitutional pitfalls. No God or gods are mentioned—not even a "being." It's just an intelligent design, clearly implying a designer of some intelligence and not much else.

Understanding ID and the refutations of it requires some familiarity with probability theory, specified complexity and other dense and daunting disciplines. The best scholarly discussion on ID that I've read is a 2001 article by Taner Edis, an assistant professor of physics at Truman State University. I found it heavy going, and it's difficult to imagine the public school biology teachers of Missouri boning up on the topic, let alone trying to stuff it in their students' ear-holes.

The truth is we don't know how the universe was created. We do know that it's taken many, many years, that species that once roamed the Earth are no more, and that many surviving species have changed over the millennia. These things—the things we know—are the things we should be teaching in public schools.

Deistic views, however they fit into the picture, are matters of faith. Those are things we should be teaching at home and at church—not in school.

When we strive to reconcile science and religion, we end up debasing both.

The Intelligent Designer is a shadowy figure indeed, a formless and incomprehensible deity that bears no resemblance whatever to the Jehovah who created the world in six days and rested on the seventh. Whatever the designer is, he is neither the Brahma hatched from the original cosmic egg nor the Olympic gods coughed up by Cronus.

No, the ID god created complex amino acids in the sure and certain knowledge that they would eventually give rise to men, women, bacteria and opossums.

But who would ever feel compelled to worship a chemical engineer? Maybe the Unitarians; most of us need something more.

What kinds of Christians are these?

LONG AGO, I LEARNED NOT TO BECOME TOO DISHEARTENED ABOUT ELECTION Day defeats, a mindset that's come in especially handy this year. The recent election set a new standard for futility: Even the Republicans I voted for lost!

What has given me a real case of the yips, though, is the reigning conventional wisdom that progressives failed to gain the presidency because they lacked Christian values, that they—we—weren't moral enough.

Honest doubts about several important details disqualify me from membership in any of the various Christian sects. But I've put in considerable Sunday school and Bible study time, not to mention two full years in a gospel band. The general principles set forth in the Holy Scriptures still strike me as a pretty good guide in matters of personal conduct.

And it seems to me that a lot of the professing Christians currently running the country mostly care about only two books of the Bible—Genesis and Revelations—and display what amounts to a go-to-hell attitude about the rest of it.

Ask a lot of red-state Christians about the meaning of "Good Samaritan," for instance, and they'll tell you the term refers to a compassionate person. And so it does. But the point of the parable was that the protagonist was a Samaritan, a nonbeliever and member of an ancient tribe distinct from the chosen people of Israel. And yet, the Lord smiled upon him because of his kindness and good will. The modern parallel would be the Good Muslim or the Good Wiccan.

The New Testament abounds with such examples. Neoconservatives believe strongly in the virtues of the marketplace, in the positive good of the immutable laws of supply and demand. Yet Jesus said it is impossible to worship both God and Mammon—the deity of money. In fact, the only time the good shepherd ever resorted to violence was when he drove the moneychangers from the Temple. This should give pause to a lot of televangelists and God-fearing CEOs, who nevertheless continue their relentless pursuit of coin to the exclusion of all else.

Many of these individuals also scoff at the idea of church-state separation, insisting that the United States is first and foremost a Christian nation. Perhaps they slept through the sermon where the preacher talked about Christ's injunction to "render unto Caesar the things that are Caesar's; and unto God the things that are God's."

Does that statement not distinguish plainly between the claims of the sacred and the secular spheres? It also seems to argue against cutting all taxes on the very wealthy, none of whom will be able to enter the kingdom of heaven—just as the camel cannot pass through the eye of a needle. Hey, don't get mad at me! It was the Savior who said it. He stuck up for tax collectors, too.

Jesus gave his biggest endorsement to the poor and the meek, objects of downright scorn from the leaders of the current conservative movement. He also talked a lot about feeding the hungry, clothing the naked and sheltering the homeless, hardly the top priorities in the Republican agenda.

Many argue these obligations are best left to private "faith-based" enterprises, which are only too happy to make the attempt using public money. News flash: In a nation of 300-plus million people, the government is the only agency that can practically address such questions as widespread hunger and affordable housing. Churches can and should help. They can't do it alone, though, not even with their federal funding and tax-exempt status. The job is simply too big for them.

By today's standards, Jesus would be judged unacceptably soft on crime. When he came upon a crowd preparing to stone a woman to death for the capital crime of adultery, he counseled mercy. His subsequent instruction to her—"Go and sin no more"—clearly indicates his faith in rehabilitation as opposed to punishment. The big liberal! It might not be stretching it too far to surmise that he probably was against the death penalty, too.

For many of our modern Christian leaders, the defining issue is the sacredness of human life, as manifested in their opposition to reproductive rights and embryonic stem cell research. They could be right about that, for all I know. It's odd, however, that they can be so adamant about the destruction of fertilized human eggs and still somehow justify the destruction of so many living, breathing Iraqi humans, who have been killed in the tens of thousands. The Bible makes no such distinction.

Yes, traditional moral values can be a tricky business. Ever since this country was born, every progressive movement has been tagged as antithetical to traditional moral values.

The whole idea of representative government was an open slap at the divine right of kings. To go against the sovereign was to go against God himself. African slavery was said to be ordained by Jehovah—the right and natural state of the sons of Ham. Every attempt to raise women above the status of chattels was deemed a defiance of the laws of God. Racial segregation, too, was and is believed by many to be the path of righteousness.

To be fair, denominations of the Christian church also gave rise to the antislavery and civil rights movements, among other harbingers of freedom and progress. Were those people anti-Christian? Were they immoral?

Well, neither are we.

Virgin Mary, the grill of my dreams

OH, HI! COME ON IN, AND PARDON THE MESS. I MUST BE A SIGHT WITH ALL THESE grease stains on my shirtfront. I've been busy in the kitchen all weekend. What have I been making? My fortune, I hope!

You hungry? I have sandwiches.

I saw this newspaper clipping, you see, about an item that sold for $28,000 on eBay: a grilled cheese sandwich with the face of the Virgin Mary. That's right, a grilled cheese sandwich that was made, kept and eventually sold by Diana Duyser of Hollywood, Fla.

She was sure the image is that of Mary because she—Duyser, that is, not Mary—won a total of $70,000 at a local casino during the 10 years the sandwich was in her home. Interestingly, the winning bidder was the online casino GoldenPalace.com, which apparently seeks to improve its odds. Those casino boys are pretty hardheaded types, so if they think those char marks are the mother of Jesus, who am I to question?

To me, the visage on the sandwich looks a lot like Rita Hayworth, whom some of you ancient history buffs might remember as a popular pinup model in the 1940s. I never pictured the Virgin Mary with full, luscious lips, heavy eyeliner and a kittenish forelock. Most depictions I've seen show her with eyes modestly downcast, hair covered and a bare minimum of makeup. But it's hard to argue with $70,000 in steady casino winnings, so maybe Botticelli had it all wrong.

You have to admit that religious iconography has changed a lot in the past few centuries. It used to be about craftsmen working with chisel and stone or canvas and palette. More recently, the faltering hand of the mortal artist has been done away with altogether. And unlike the days when Michelangelo spent as much time seeking the flawless block of marble as he did in sculpting it, the modern materials tend to be pretty prosaic.

How things change! In 1978, Mario Rubio burned a tortilla in such a way as to depict a bearded, mournful face that drew more than 8,000 pilgrims to her rural New Mexico home. In 1980, a crucified Christ was miraculously rendered by streetlight reflections and shadows of a shrub and a real-estate sign on a California garage door. Thousands of gawkers gathered to view a rust-stained chimney of a suburban Chicago bowling alley in 1987. That same year, a stained freezer door on the porch of a mobile home in Gallatin, Tenn., attracted as many as 3,000 onlookers for several nights running until the annoyed owner unscrewed the porch light bulb. Subsequently, the savior appeared on the gnarled trunk of a sycamore in New Haven, Conn.; on a linoleum tabletop in Harris Country, Tex.; in a dirty double-paned window in New York City.

The foregoing is just a partial list of real-life examples. None of them approaches the grilled cheese sandwich for cost, convenience or ease of shipping and handling. As for sheer durability, remember that Duyser managed to milk her Mary at the slots and blackjack tables for 10 years before she unloaded it—mold-free!—for a cool $28K.

But you have to do the thing right. Researchers have found the longest-lasting grilled cheese sandwiches are generously slathered with margarine or some I-can't-believe-it's-really-grease sort of substance, which are rich in something called trans-fats. Fungi don't like trans-fats, anymore than they like store-bought, pre-sliced white bread loaded with preservatives like sorbic acid and propionic acid. They don't call it "Wonder Bread" for nothing. And processed cheese-food product is high in calcium and slightly acidic, endowing it with significant mold-retardant properties.

Sure you don't want a sandwich?

Anyway, with those easily available materials, a long weekend and a heapin' helping of faith and optimism, I was pretty sure I could grill a miracle on a par with that of Duyser, and I wouldn't hold out for a gross of $98,000, like she did. I'm not greedy. I was willing to settle for maybe $10,000 per sandwich, which would still net me a tidy profit. I also planned to haul the surplus, non-miraculous sandwiches down to the food bank as a kind of cosmic exchange, but it turned out they didn't want 'em.

So, I've been working the griddle and two frying pans for four days now without a single recognizable religious figure. My faith is beginning to get a little charred at the edges.

Not that the effort hasn't yielded some worthwhile results. This sandwich here looks just like Snuffy Smith; see the smoke coming out of his little pipe? You're looking at it upside down! And here, this one looks like the famous picture of the Grassy Knoll. You can just make out the guy with the rifle crouching in the bushes. You can't? Well, what about this one—it looks just like that actor, Jason Alexander, doesn't it? Yeah, come to think of it, Jason Alexander does look a little bit like a grilled cheese sandwich.

Sure you're not hungry? Then, how about a drink?

Great. Make mine a double.

There's no piety deficit in U.S. politics

POLITICIANS IN OUR SUPPOSEDLY SECULAR REPUBLIC HAVE NEVER HESITATED TO invoke the almighty in their own causes, righteous or otherwise. While our founders, rationalists to a man, might have despised the divine right of kings, they did not flinch from giving due credit to divine providence.

Rhetorically, very little has changed in the ensuing centuries. In fact, it seems as though the conflation of the stump and the pulpit is greater than ever before. There is definitely no sanctimony deficit.

The inaugural speeches this month were heavily larded with pious references, with President George W. Bush lauding Jehovah as "the author of liberty" and newly elected Gov. Matt Blunt offering the bold proposition that religious values should be "embraced, not scorned."

The governor's statement might lead one to believe that other politicians openly scoff at religion, an inference that is hardly true. Even New York Sen. Hillary Clinton—believed by many to be the wife of Satan himself—said last week that religious people must be allowed to "live out their faith in the public square."

The prospect of public squares being overrun with bawling preachers, fly-by-night prophets and pandering politicians strikes me as an excellent argument for avoiding public places altogether. I'd rather stay home and watch infomercials.

Nevertheless, I can't argue with the proposition that individuals ought to be able to express their opinions, religious or otherwise, openly and without fear of government interference.

Toleration must be extended not just to the powerful officeholders, and that, of course, is where the trouble begins. It extends also to the guy with the wild beard and the sign that proclaims, "The end is near," to the Hare Krishna with their saffron robes and comical topknots, to the mullah who reads aloud from the Quran and to the redneck deacon who claims uppity women and racial mixing are abominations in the sight of God.

To those who say religion and politics don't mix, I say, what on Earth are you talking about? Religion has been part and parcel of almost every significant political conflict in our nation's history.

Both the anti-slavery and pro-slavery movements, for example, relied on Scripture to bolster their respective positions. The civil rights revolution of the 1960s would never have happened but for the ability of black churches to organize for political purposes. Prohibition proceeded directly from the church-driven temperance movement. The Cold War was fueled largely by fears of godless communism.

To protest against religion in politics is as futile as raging against the tide. And yet so much of the political religiosity on parade appears to be simple pandering. Usually when a person running for office possesses unquestioned credentials as a sincere, practicing Christian—such as those possessed by failed gubernatorial candidate the Rev. Larry Rice—that person gets clobbered in the polls.

It is probably for the best, however, that the religious rhetoric from politicians amounts mostly to lip service. While it is altogether right and proper to employ one's religion as a general moral compass in policy-making, trying to impose it literally is almost always a grave mistake—counterproductive as well as unconstitutional.

For instance, those who want public schools to organize prayer sessions are, ironically, often the same people who believe any government undertaking is doomed to failure. They think the government can't run Social Security, can't effectively protect the environment, feed the hungry or house the homeless.

And yet they appear eager for government institutions—namely public schools—to take an active role in the religious education of their children, not to mention yours and mine. I can't understand how anyone would want to leave such a crucial matter in the hands of government. The founders understood this.

Or consider the efforts of some to have the Ten Commandments displayed at county courthouses. Supporters cite Deuteronomy 6:9—"And thou shalt write them upon the posts of thy house, and on thy gates"—to justify what is plainly the sort of establishment of religion forbidden by the Constitution.

Here, I think, there could be room for compromise. The first four commandments are obviously sect-specific and therefore unsuitable for the courthouse. The next four amount to general rules of conduct.

Only the last two are strictly applicable to the courthouse setting. The warning about bearing false witness is a warning to would-be perjurers. The last commandment, discouraging covetousness, could conceivably reduce the number of lawsuits filed and free up the dockets considerably. But these are purely practical matters, and besides, I don't think thou are supposed to pick and choose among the commandments.

For the most part, it's probably better that religion in politics remain rhetorical. In the beginning was the word, and to this day the word can instruct and inspire our citizens and our leaders, even if it's a dubious basis for public policy.

Neither science nor faith answers the ultimate question

IT'S A CARNIVAL; IT'S A BEACH; IT'S A VEIL OF TEARS AND NOT A BED OF ROSES. IT might be charmed, still, high and low. It imitates art, it's too short and Coke adds it.

And after all this jabber, we still don't know the meaning of life. It is a discussion that until relatively recently was confined mostly to poets and philosophers, those who delve into the mysteries. Now it has entered the prosaic realm of politicians and lawyers, a suitable subject for legislation and litigation at every level.

The change is largely a result of advancing technology. Human life can now be created in a laboratory, and it can be prolonged almost indefinitely by methods that are every bit as artificial. Clearly, there is no consensus as to where it begins, where it ends and what it means.

Consider the case of Terri Schiavo, the Florida woman who has lingered in a vegetative state for more than 15 years. Her husband says she long ago expressed her wish not to live under such circumstances, and for years he has sought legal permission to remove her feeding tube.

Her parents are equally convinced that their daughter would have wanted to live, and aided by conservative religious groups, they continue the battle to keep her breathing—alive in the same sense that a pithed frog is alive. Ultimately, the court ruling will rest not on what constitutes life or meaningful life but instead on whether life-and-death decisions are up to spouses or to parents.

What Schiavo is thinking, if anything, none may know. That's not the case in Oregon, where the law allows dying people of sound mind to choose physician-assisted suicide. No mind-reading required here, only adherence to the clearly expressed wishes of the terminally ill.

The U.S. Department of Justice is attempting to overturn the state's assisted suicide law, arguing that the extra bump of morphine that eases the suffering patient over the mortal hump constitutes a misuse of federally controlled substances. The U.S. Supreme Court is scheduled to decide the case in its upcoming session.

The issue of suffering and the end of life has taken on particular relevance to the Catholic Church as Pope John Paul II approaches the end of his allotted span. The pontiff suffers from Parkinson's disease, respiratory problems and agonizing aches in every joint.

There's no question that JP2 is determined to remain alive as long as possible. In his message for Lent, he condemned the "current mentality" that considers people "almost useless when they are reduced in their capacities due to the difficulties of age or sickness." The Vatican newspaper compared his infirmities to the suffering of Jesus Christ on the cross and compared "the bed of pain" to "the cathedral of life."

One might admire the courage and convictions of the man and still recognize that to many people, including me, terminal agony is in no way ennobling.

With a few notable exceptions, the value of a human life lies more in the way it is conducted than the means by which it is ended.

At the other end of the continuum rages the debate about where human life begins. To a lot of people, the instant an ovum is fertilized, it becomes a human life as precious and sacred as that of Jessica Lunsford or Vice President Dick Cheney. Some folks consider even preventive birth control to be an act of homicide—a denial of life.

Naturally, such people oppose all stem cell research, which uses the undifferentiated human cells found in undeveloped embryos. Few believe such research would not lead to breakthroughs in the treatment of myriad ailments, such as diabetes, Parkinson's and paralysis. They simply don't think it's worth the sacrifice of a single blessed blastula.

Last month, their worst fears were realized when the British scientist who cloned Dolly the sheep was granted a license to clone human embryos for research purposes. Ian Wilmut said his experiments will focus on Lou Gehrig's disease, the nerve disorder that has taken many lives and destroyed many others.

Wilmut and his colleagues emphasize that therapeutic cloning does not result in babies. The embryonic cell clusters never reach the point of consciousness or individuality because they are kept for no more than 14 days.

Well, that's the problem, say the opponents, who are at least theologically consistent in their thinking. But there's a big difference between "theologically" and "logically."

Consider the matter logically, and there's no way a cluster of a dozen undifferentiated cells is the same thing as a living, breathing baby. As part of the natural course of things, many early embryos are spontaneously aborted, and often, such miscarriages are not even noticed, let alone mourned.

To equate a fertilized ovum with the life of a newborn child does not affirm life; it cheapens it. To say the life of a brain-dead person is as meaningful as that of a fully cognizant human being is a willful denial of obvious realities. To keep painfully sick people artificially alive against their own wishes is an act that borders on the cruel.

Technology has made infinitely more complicated the discussions about the meaning of life. But as we discuss, let us bear one thing in mind: We still devote far fewer technological resources to prolonging or creating human lives than we do to ending them.

Let the pro-life forces paste that in their hats.

"I treasure a photograph of me standing next to Monroe," Forrest wrote in one of his columns. "He is the very model of dignified bearing. I look like someone is tickling my feet." Forrest played briefly with Bill Monroe's band, the Bluegrass Boys, in the mid-1980s. "In all the years I knew Forrest," says photographer John Trotter, "I only saw him at a loss for words twice; this was one of the times."

CHAPTER 3

NOTES ON MUSIC AND SOCIETY

Fiddlin' around on stage offers fix for bass junkie

WHEN THE FIRST WAVES HIT YOUR BRAIN, THE DIZZY ECSTASY SEEMS SO INNOCENT, providing a few fleeting moments of unbounded pleasure. But this pernicious thing quickly embraces and then seizes its victims until their craving for more and more and even more becomes a consuming obsession.

Crack? Who's talking about crack? I am speaking of performing.

Performing is the only way to get applause, which is actually a highly concentrated form of approval. Approval is medically safe and easily available from mothers, pets and small children. Applause is more dangerous and tougher to kick.

I've been there, man. Ever since I first beat my spoon on the high chair, I wanted to be a performer. I became so addicted that I quit college to launch a five-year career as a penniless bassman in a country-blues band, till hunger drove me back to a day job.

Since then, I've been like a cunning alcoholic, sneaking gigs on the side for an occasional fix but otherwise shuddering with withdrawal pangs. A week ago, though, I got a mainline dose that's put that monkey right back on my back.

The Old Hound Dog from KOPN called me to say some big-note musicians were going to play at the Missouri Theater and wouldn't mind if some of the local talent stood up with them. The performers were Vassar Clements, John McEuen, Rodney Dillard and Hans Olson. Those names might not ring a bell with many people, but they play on about 20 of my favorite albums.

The afternoon before the show, I went down to the theater, lugging my bass fiddle and wearing my stylish "stingy-brim" fedora. McEuen, who was testing the microphones, saw this strange creature trudging up the aisle and hollered: "Hey, you—Ed Norton with the bass. Get up here."

Getting up there, I struggled through a sound check with McEuen on guitar and banjo, Dillard on guitar and vocals and Olson on harmonica. Clements had already come and gone.

When McEuen told me he "could use you on a few songs tonight," I was loony with excitement. My joy was only slightly marred by the fact that there weren't enough microphones to go around and I would have to play without one. "Just hit it hard," McEuen advised.

By curtain time, I was as nervous as a Quaker bride, and my usual icy sang-froid crumbled completely when I met Vassar Clements.

Let me explain about Vassar. His back-beat, bluesy fiddling style has been imitated by almost every aspiring young fiddler in the last 25 years. What John Coltrane did for jazz saxophonists, Vassar did for country fiddlers. Finding myself face to face with this demigod, the best I could manage was to ask him what he'd been up to lately.

"Opened up some ice cream stores," he answered. "That didn't work. Lost a pile of money, so I'm back doing this." I loyally asserted that I would've given him all my ice cream custom if I'd ever seen one of his stores. But I couldn't help hinking that the loss to the cold-licks industry was a big boost for the hot-licks business.

Propped up between my musical idols, I played the show in a sort of awed tupor. Fortunately, country bass isn't complicated; mostly you just stand up here and play:

Lub...dub...lub...dub...

The end of the show was approaching, and I hadn't noticeably shamed myself, when Vassar turned to me and said, "Take a ride on the bridge the second time go around." A solo.

And I almost pulled it off. Going into a syncopated slap rhythm, I was attempting to end the bass break with a complicated cross-string maneuver—when I missed the string. Where the grand final note of the solo should have ounded, there was empty air.

The musicians courteously didn't mention it. They just packed up their gear after the show, said "Good job, sonny" and left.

I had almost convinced myself that no one noticed when an old and slightly deaf acquaintance who'd been in the balcony asked me: "The uh, hesitation hing you did at the end," he said. "Was that on purpose?"

Since then, I've been busy with plans to open up a chain of frozen taco stands. Still, if you hear of any big talent agencies who are hot to sign this previously obscure bass player with the hesitating style, tell 'em to ring me up.

I need a fix in the worst way.

Simulation stimulation is the brain wave of the future

SOMETHING HAPPENED THIS SUMMER THAT MIGHT CARRY THE BIGGEST POTENTIAL for good or evil since the concept of majority rule, and it got barely a mention on the evening news.

The epochal event to which I refer is the announcement by a computer scientist that he has developed a video game that will stimulate the same areas of the brain that are stimulated during sex. The network news' anchorwoman said that, apparently, the idea is that activating those precise areas of the cerebral cortex will produce a feeling akin to sexual climax.

After that briefest of synopses, the heartless newscaster moved on to an entirely different patch of brain cells—the boring, non-sexy ones that deal with things like banking crises and oil spills. Even her severely abridged report, however, opens up endless fields of speculation about the brand-new area of computer-simulated sex.

One wonders, does the terminal display symmetrical patterns like Herr Dr. Rorshcach's famous inkblot test, probing the dark and incomprehensible wrinkles and recesses of the mind? Or is it just a series of multiple choice queries, starting with blond, brunette or redhead?

I know little about computers, and my premedical training was cut short in the ninth grade when I found out it would require me to take a math course. But any fool who knows a superior parietal lobule from an intraparietal sulcus can tell you that scientists long ago pinpointed which areas of gray matter affect what sensory functions.

It follows that certain aspects of brain function are inseparable from the act of sex. Certainly, sex is partly visual. The genius who's concocted the new, computerized sex must have made startling improvements over the little Nintendo man, who, while nifty, is no one's idea of a sex symbol.

And the machine must titillate that part of the brain devoted to tactile sensation—another essential part of the sex sensation. Does the computer ask the user to select one texture from a list, perhaps? Bunny's nose, moss-covered rock, warm piecrust, Vaseline on velvet? …

The senses of taste, smell and hearing also play their parts in exciting lust, and each can be correlated with a small, specific patch of gray matter.

Gee, that's five areas already, and we haven't even gotten into the fine motor skills necessary to unhooking, unzipping and French kissing.

OK, for the sake of argument, let's concede that the technology exists to stimulate the sex-oriented areas of the brain via a computer program. Assuming it can be done, it could present great dangers to the poor lonely hearts who plug in.

A tiny programming error—the malfunctioning of a single microchip— could lead to disaster. If the wrong brain cells get massaged, some innocent thrill-seeker could find himself afflicted with chronic drooling or a permanent leg twitch, like a pithed frog with an electrode applied.

It could lead to a whole new form of auto-eroticism, as heedless youths start wiring their sconces into the IBM and "hacking off" behind closed doors. And what happens when the system goes down?

The idea is undeniably fascinating, and I, for one, will certainly keep a keen lookout for further news flashes. At heart, though, I'm utterly unconvinced that computer sex will make any serious inroads into the traditional methods. Some of us like our software the old-fashioned way.

Humor, like art, is in the eye of the beholder

LENNY BRUCE, WHEREVER HE IS, MUST BE HAVING A GOOD LAUGH RIGHT NOW.

The acquittal of the rap group 2 Live Crew signals another tentative step of our society toward healthy tolerance. At least, things are better than they were in Bruce's day.

About three decades ago, the late comedian was arrested after a show and charged with obscenity because he used "dirty" words in his routines. In court, Bruce wept in anger and frustration as a monotonic police officer recited his words to an unamused jury. Bruce was convicted, and it broke him.

During 2 Live Crew's trial on obscenity charges last week, a bailiff found the jurors in the hall during a recess doubled up with laughter. "They were cracking up," she said. "One of them was laughing so hard he could hardly breathe."

The hilarity stemmed from the prosecution's attempts to prove 2 Live Crew's live show was obscene. Over and over, the state blared an unintelligible tape of the performance as a red-faced sheriff's deputy deciphered it from the witness stand.

The jurors reached their verdict quickly: Not guilty. "We found many of the things very humorous," one said afterward. "Our feelings were, the musicians in the band were telling the public how they felt inside of themselves, and they were doing it with music. We thought it had some art in it."

Censorship was also slapped down this month in Cincinnati. A jury there found an art museum curator not guilty of charges that he broke obscenity statutes by displaying sexually explicit photographs by the late Robert Mapplethorpe.

Even in uptight Cincy, people weren't buying the crazy notion that the exhibit "pandered to the prurient interest"—a legal term that means getting people all hot and bothered and thus more likely to become serial rapists.

The folks who went to view Mapplethorpe's photos are members of the "art crowd," a serious bunch that doesn't normally frequent peep shows. Not being an artsy type myself, I don't know what they liked about five photographs of men in erotic and sadomasochistic poses. But I'm betting not a single gallery patron was panting, leering or foaming at the mouth.

Despite the acquittals, there are those who would say censorship of the arts remains an ever-growing menace. The National Endowment for the Arts stands accused of supporting "obscene" works, and some politicians would like to pull all funding for the federal arts agency.

To hear Sen. Jesse Helms and his allies talk about it, you'd think the NEA did nothing but subsidize repulsive projects. Two examples are brought up repeatedly: One is a picture of a cross in a jar of urine; the other is an American flag on the floor of a gallery, inviting the public to tread on Old Glory.

In truth, the agency backs plenty of wholesome, uplifting activities as well. For instance, Fulton resident Mabel Murphy, 83, netted a $5,000 NEA grant last year for her outstanding quilts. And the annual fiddling and folk music onvention at Bethel is partly funded with NEA money. In those cases, art is omething to delight the eye and set the toe to tapping.

But that cannot be the only function of art. Picasso's paintings outraged onvention in the early part of this century. Dali's surrealism jarred tender ensibilities, and Nijinksy's sensuous dancing scandalized even the worldly Parisians. If all the NEA did was award grants for two "offensive" artworks, it's a oretty tame organization.

In the wake of the two obscenity trials, perhaps Helms and his congressional cohorts will wake up to the fact that the arts are better left unfettered. If a few oeople are offended, well, that's the price of freedom. It doesn't come without a ight.

And amid the hue and cry, don't be alarmed if you hear a ghostly chuckle. t's only Lenny Bruce having the last laugh.

Musical revisionism strikes a false note

MULTICULTURAL REVISIONISM—THE CASTING OF HISTORY FROM A NON-WHITE perspective—is one of the healthiest trends in our ongoing political dialogue. It's like airing out the house: Every once in awhile, you've got to do it even if you let a few flies in during the process.

For instance, on the 500th anniversary of Columbus' historic voyage, I applauded those who painted him as a pop-eyed psychopath, a madman whose mission in life was to enslave and brutalize native populations. OK, the interpretation might have been a teensy bit skewed, but after half a millennium of uninterrupted adulation for the old boy, it was time to let the other side have its shout.

There are limits, however, to the white-man-as-villain theory of history. I become downright reactionary whenever I hear the by-now-familiar contention that white musicians "stole" rock 'n' roll from African-Americans.

Such statements betray a woeful unfamiliarity with music, especially popular music. Although musicians themselves are apt to say, "I stole that lick from so-and-so," they aren't drawing a moral conclusion; they're acknowledging a musical debt.

Music transcends the issues of race and politics even as it encompasses them. Once one starts making allegations of cultural larceny, almost every musician and style of music is to some degree guilty.

The most frequent target of this charge is Elvis Presley, a gorgeous white boy whose vocal stylings were modeled on black singers of his day. He became a pop idol while most of them slipped into obscurity.

Unfair? Probably. It still might be instructive to remember that Presley's "Hound Dog," which he is said to have stolen from a black blues singer, was written by a white man. So was the album's B-side, "Blue Moon of Kentucky," by Bill Monroe, the father of bluegrass music. Monroe, in turn, credits black blues singer Arnold Schultz as his biggest musical influence.

And so it goes, back to some hunched-over, prehensile humanoid who figured out how to knock two sticks together to make a pleasing click, which Elvis later stole.

By the mid-1950s, "race music," so called, could no longer be kept from the white mass market. The stuff was too compelling, too powerful to be contained. Elvis was a talented crooner who caught the wave, and it's safe to say that in the intervening few decades, black-white integration has been successfully achieved in the pop music field.

The racial roots of popular music are so intertwined as to be nearly untraceable. Consider: J.S. Bach is credited with devising the 12-tone scale— do, re, me, etc.—upon which most Western music is based. A few centuries later, when Joe "King" Oliver inflamed New Orleans audiences with his "jass" music, he relied on that same musical structure Bach used. And he did it on the trumpet, an instrument that came not from Africa but from Europe. Yet, no sane person would accuse Oliver of creative pilfering. He was a true original, a pioneer, a genius.

The five-string banjo is mainly used for hillbilly music, and black hillbilly banjo players are as rare as blue rubies. Still, there is no denying that the instrument's antecedent were African in origin. When the white sons and daughters of Appalachia appropriated it, did they do wrong? Was it ethnic trespassing?

Some people, back in the '30s, thought it odd that Charlie Christian and Benny Goodman recorded together. Hearing those cuts today, the pigmentation of the players recedes into insignificance beside the magnificent swing and soul of the music itself.

Then came rock 'n' roll. Try as they might, the white racists were unable to stop the musical melding, or even slow it down. The radical revisionists' attempts to condemn it retroactively are almost as wrong, and equally futile.

Dress codes' dictates can't halt fashion trend

EVER SINCE YAHWEH ORDERED ADAM AND EVE TO GET SOME CLOTHES ON AND get out of the garden, authority and adolescence have clashed over what constitutes proper dress. Some of you older boys might recall rebuckling your knickerbockers below the knee in a presumptuous imitation of man's long trousers—a practice much frowned up on by late Victorian graybeards.

Now, the age-old conflict is being re-enacted in Columbia schools with dress codes that forbid "gang" attire such as droopy pants and red or blue bandannas.

Like all age-old conflicts, this one is not as simple as it might at first appear. A bandanna no more makes a kid a criminal than a leather jacket makes a newspaper writer a bomber pilot, but there is something to school officials' contention that such fashions are rooted in the criminal milieu. For instance, the sagging pants style began in prison, where belts are denied and trousers sag naturally.

The anti-gang dress code, which has been in effect for several months, doesn't seem particularly drastic. Moreover, school officials and students interviewed by Tribune reporters agreed the regulations were not rigidly enforced. "We try not to make a big deal out of it," Blue Ridge Elementary principal David Brunda said.

A Jefferson Junior High eight-grader said he usually isn't hassled about his clothing. But he resents what he sees as a double standard: "They won't let us wear our clothes, but they let the skinheads wear their big-ass boots."

He makes an excellent point. At this stage, the black students are most likely to emulate the inner-city "gang" look. It seems questionable to suppress only those fashions, especially at a time when the Columbia School District has announced its intention to promote multicultural diversity.

What better example of it exists than the multiplicity of clothing styles students wear to school every day? Unless you expect to persuade the students to dress up in dashikis or kilts or lederhosen to display pride in their diverse cultural backgrounds. Good luck with that program.

In a letter to parents announcing the dress code, West Boulevard Elementary School cited some students' "preoccupation" with gangland fashion, advising parents to watch out for "unusual items of clothing" like plaid shirts with only the top button fastened.

School officials are absolutely correct to inform parents about such things. It is properly a family matter what clothes a kid wears to school, and the parents need to know what's going on.

Preoccupation with fashion, however, has always been present among grade school students. My sense is that they don't want to join a gang so much as they want to be part of the crowd. For example, if the most popular girls start wearing rag-wool sweaters, a good many other girls will decide nothing else will do but the exact same sweater. If the coolest boy suddenly starts wearing his ball cap brim to one side, they'll all be doing it by end of the school day.

Capitalism, along with conformism, is the powerful driving force of multiculturalism. The American ideal is to seek out something new, different and daring—and sell the blazes out of it. If a thing is successfully mass-marketed, the novelty inevitably dissipates and the shock passes. Popular fashions, no matter how outrageous they seem at the outset, usually work their way into the mainstream.

Consider: Before T-shirts became ubiquitous, they were symbols of rebellion. Hippie styles were startling for awhile—until even fat, old politicians let their sideburns grow and their hair cover their ears. The unnerving punk fashions of the '70s were neatened up and repackaged with spectacular success as a palatable "New Wave." Our big, friendly culture gobbles up diversity and regurgitates it in neat, marketable units.

Columbia schools might be well advised to sit back and let multicultural capitalism do its work. The so-called "gang" styles are already available at malls everywhere. The more common and trendy they become, the less they signify criminality.

By and by, straight-A students will be seen sporting red and blue bandannas. Chemists will start buttoning only the top buttons of their plaid shirts. Sears will announce a new line of "Street-smart 'Baggy Britches' for Dad 'n' lad." Jerry Brown will campaign in an Oakland Raiders warmup jacket.

By then, of course, the students will have gone on to something else. And the schools would have to devise a whole new dress code.

Society take notice: Women have lock on genetic codes

WOMEN. GIVE 'EM A SINGLE INCH, AND THEY END UP WITH THE WHOLE DOUBLE helix.

Dispassionate observers are bound to acknowledge biological differences between the genders. Besides the coarsely obvious ones, I mean. For instance, men tend to be bigger and stronger than women, with a highly evolved aptitude for power tools. Women, in contrast, are inclined to be more developed from the brain stem up, with a gift for grasping abstractions and subtleties, which eludes most men, plus a superior eye for color.

Only in the past few generations have we begun to realize that individual variations and circumstances render such generalizations meaningless. Accordingly, women are finally demanding their long overdue status as co-equals in the political, economic and domestic spheres.

Last week, there came to my attention a scientific fact about the differences between woman and man. Heretofore unknown to me, it could change the whole way we view womankind and her role in the world.

I came across the item in an Associated Press story about some locks of hair believed to have been snipped from the head of George Washington. FBI scientists, the story said, will examine 11 snippets of hair reputed to have come from the head of George Washington.

The scientists will analyze "the mitrochondrial DNA, or genetic building blocks that lie outside the cell nucleus," the story explained. Thanks to the miracle of DNA decoding, scientists will be able to match the ancient locks with hair samples from two direct descendants of the first president.

My first thought was that if 11 samples of Washington's hair are still around nearly two centuries after his death, it at least explains why he had to wear a wig. Apparently, he could hardly turn around without encountering some fawning admirer waving a pair of shears and asking to snip off a keepsake.

"It's actually for a friend," they would say as The Father of Our Country submitted stoically to the indignities of his celebrity.

Buried deep in the background text, I found the crucial fact: "Only daughters pass on the specific code sequence to the next generation," the story said. "If there had not been a daughter in every generation of the Washington family, the line would have ended."

The two gentlewomen, ages 67 and 70—whose hair the FBI will use for purposes of comparison—are direct matrilineal descendants: daughters of daughters of daughters of daughters of daughters of the daughter of Betty Washington Lewis, George's sister.

The fact that women alone are the intergenerational transmitters of the genetic code came as a bombshell to me. No doubt every 9-year-old gets taught that stuff now, but when I was a lad there was no such thing as DNA.

From time immemorial, we've been led to regard direct ancestral lineage as primarily a male thing, passed on from father to son. It has been the foundation of law and custom from earliest times. Land, wealth and titles were passed from fathers to sons. Daughters, considered little more than chattel, were to be married off as quickly as possible. Once wed, a woman's main function was to bear and raise as many male children as possible. Otherwise, the thinking went, the line would die out.

To this day, the myth persists. In our own society, it perseveres in the expectation that women will forsake their own names for those of their husbands. It endures in the heartfelt but misguided wish of many couples that they be granted a son rather than a daughter.

When you think about it, a matrilineal system is perfectly logical. Whenever a child is born, the mother's identity is a far more certain thing than the father's. Nevertheless, the fact that genetic continuity depends on the woman is a direct challenge and refutation to the patriarchal assumptions that have always governed human society. Insofar as cultural implications, it's right on a par with the discovery that Earth revolves around the sun.

Granted, I might have misunderstood the scientific concepts involved. If another Associated Press story is to be believed, I almost certainly did. A spokesman for something called the International Center for the Advancement of Science Literacy said only one-fifth of Americans know enough about DNA to understand a newspaper story about it. What's more, the same story quoted a survey to the effect that only 17 percent regarded newspapers as a trustworthy source of information in the first place.

But on the off chance that I savvy the gist, I wish to advance a modest proposal to the DNA scientists who are probably busy this very moment figuring out how to clone George Washington. My advice is: Forget about him. Clone Betty Washington instead. Because there's one fact you don't need to find out from a newspaper: Male geese don't lay golden eggs.

MU artist's work at fair misunderstood by officials

THE OLD STATE FAIR, SHE AIN'T WHAT SHE USED TO BE, AIN'T WHAT SHE USED TO be many long years ago.

I wax lyrical every time I think about the fair and its great displays of pies, preserves, garden produce and livestock on the hoof. Not to mention the Garden of Eden tent.

The Garden of Eden tent at the Iowa State Fair was where I received one of my first tastes of sin some decades ago—it doesn't matter how many. My buddy Joe and I each paid a buck to enter the tent and see the exotic dancers. They'll take you all the way back to the garden!" the shill promised. As it turned out, the program left our curiosity more stimulated than satisfied, and we anted up another buck to go into an adjoining tent for a peek at "Bobby—half male, half female. A true freak of nature!"

Bobby turned out to be a horse. The carnival man invited us to bend down and check out the goods, but we felt we'd learned enough valuable lessons already that day.

Maybe this musty memory is the reason I can't imagine the state fair as the strict guardian of public morals. At this year's Missouri State Fair, the really heavy BBs came down not in the cattle barn but in the fine arts exhibition.

The Missouri Arts Council's executive director pulled one of the pieces from the prestigious Missouri Top 50 exhibit. He was afraid the work by MU student Andy Davis would give offense to fairgoers.

The controversial work is titled "The Honor System." It's a 4-by-5-foot chunk of wall with a coat rack attached and on the rack hang a man's coat and hat, a woman's coat and his-'n'-her chastity belts.

"The chastity belts were supposed to make you think of mental attitudes that one should adopt when you leave the house for the day," David told a Tribune reporter. He wondered how a piece that celebrated marital fidelity could become so controversial.

The symbolism is obvious enough that even a newspaper editor could grasp its implications. But arts council director Anthony Radich apparently was concerned the message would be misconstrued. He advised state fair officials to pull the work and avoid potential controversy over public arts funding.

"The state fair would have been deeply criticized for being insensitive to their audience," Radich said in defense of his decision. "We should be sensitive to what the audience is: families and young people."

In trying to imagine how anyone would be scandalized by "The Honor System," I was forced to conclude that most impressionable young people would not have recognized the chastity belts for what they are. I wasn't sure myself until I read the caption. It just looked like a hat-and-coat ensemble oddly juxtaposed with ornate jockstraps.

Assume I'm strolling through the exhibit with my highly impressionable 5-year-old son, and he sees "The Honor System," stops, points and says, "What are those?"

"Goat harnesses, I guess." I would be prompt. "Or maybe sling-shots. I dunno. Let's move on." A brief display of stony philistinism probably would quall any further questioning. In any event, I can't envision the sort of crisis scenario that apparently appears to Radich in his nightmares.

A ready compromise was available, had Radich chosen to accept it. Gary Noland, the fair's resident artist this year, made space in his room for "The Honor System" and posted a sign at the exhibit inviting people in to view it. Ordered to take the work down, he resigned his post and—this is impressive— gave up his $750 stipend.

"If the arts agencies aren't going to be sticking by the artists, the arts have to stick up for themselves," Noland declared.

Artists, heed his words. Advocates like Radich, who concern themselves primarily with not offending imaginary knuckleheads, might not fully represent your views and interests. Maybe they'd be better employed promoting some other sort of products line: goat harnesses, maybe, or slingshots. Something where free expression is not a fundamental concern.

Although "The Honor System" wasn't even a close call, Radich and other public arts administrators find themselves in a difficult spot. They have to fight the current fictions that arts money is a major financial burden, and that most of it goes to scoffers, deviates and radicals.

The harshest critics of the National Endowment for the Arts are still bringing up that cross-in-the-urine motif that so outraged everyone about 10 years ago. That work and the flag on the floor are cited constantly, and it badly distorts the debate about public arts funding. Those works were not typical examples of where the money was going.

My experiences with NEA-sponsored activities were far more representational. The annual Bethel Fiddle Convention, at its height, was a three-day affair. It brought together young and old, rural and urban, rich and poor for fiddling workshops, concerts, contests, dances and demonstrations. And then there was the charming old lady in Fulton who fashioned the most astoundingly gorgeous patchwork quilts I'd ever seen in my life. She received an NEA grant to conduct quilting bees, where she passed her art and techniques on to the next generation.

I applaud these wise uses of the tax dollar. And I accept the fact that some NEA money goes to things like modern dance, experimental opera and maybe even to visual artists with aggressive attitudes, though I'm interested in none of these things.

I'm even less interested in the B-1 bomber, Star Wars and biological weapons research, which eat up a far bigger portion of the federal tax dollar than the NEA does in its wildest fantasies.

Now that's offensive. So is the concept that art must not offend, that art must avoid criticism. That's not art. That's politics.

Bluegrass father Bill Monroe took love for music to grave

IN CASE ANYBODY'S KEEPING TRACK, THE WORLD HAS ONE LESS LIVING LEGEND than it did last week. Bill Monroe, who died a few years shy of his 85th birthday, was the real deal.

Legends don't happen along just every day. Oh, there are plenty of mere celebrities—one-hit wonders and talentless shills such as John Tesh or Vanna White.

Monroe made a lasting mark on the world by inventing a new kind of music. The origins of rock 'n' roll are endlessly disputed. And several geniuses could claim to have come up with the rudiments of what we call jazz. But no one ever argued with the fact that Monroe was the father of bluegrass.

Music historians rank him with McKinley Morganfield, aka Muddy Waters, the barefoot plantation hand who eventually forged the American urban blues style. I played briefly with Monroe's band, the Bluegrass Boys, in the mid-1980s, and it remains the highlight of my somewhat checkered musical career. I treasure a photograph of me standing next to Monroe. He is the very model of dignified bearing. I look like someone is tickling my feet.

Mr. Bill, as he liked to be called, had a keen sense of his own accomplishments and his contributions to American culture. The old gentleman was given to occasional grandiose pronouncements such as: "Bluegrass music is the most popular music in the world," and "Bluegrass is where rock 'n' roll got its timing."

Overstatements, no doubt, but not as outrageous as you might think. Monroe's music was performed and applauded from deepest Appalachia to the Far East to Switzerland to South Africa. Listen to the early rockabilly guitar riffs and compare them to Monroe's mandolin stylings on numbers like "Get Up John." The similarities are striking.

Like many great men, Monroe had flaws that almost matched his mighty gifts. He was reputed to be tyrannical toward band members, tight with money and a ferocious womanizer.

He had a sweetheart in every town, and each one would bring him a pie and another one for the Bluegrass Boys. His spurned girlfriends were constant sources of aggravation. One of them once smashed his mandolin, and another so harried and harassed him in 1986—when he was 75—that he clouted her upside the head with a Bible. Misdemeanor assault charges against him were later dropped.

Despite his enduring popularity, he was constantly short of cash. It was one reason he kept touring until the last days of his life. It was not, however, the only reason.

When I played with the Bluegrass Boys, it was evident to me that Monroe literally lived for performing. Away from the stage lights, he seemed feeble, addled and distant. With a mandolin in his hand and an audience or a pretty girl in front of him, he became the most youthful septuagenarian I'd ever seen.

There's an old joke about the bluegrass picker who died and was standing in front of the pearly gates when he heard some bluesy mandolin music emanating from within. He exclaimed: "Why, that sounds like Bill Monroe!"

"Nope, that's God," St. Peter replied. "He just thinks he's Bill Monroe."

I'd like to think Mr. Bill's up there now, playing duets. And I bet he's taking the leads.

HMO refuses to cover cost of artificial ardor

THE NATION'S LARGEST HEALTH MANAGEMENT ORGANIZATION ANNOUNCED LAST week that it would not cover the cost of Viagra, the male potency pill that Leno, Letterman and thousands of other American men say is the best thing that's ever happened to them. The HMO maintains the cost, at $10 a dose, is too much.

Ordinarily, a news item about an HMO refusing coverage to patients would make me outraged at the greed of such a flint-hearted organization. Not this time. In a world of scarce resources, male sex drive supplementation ought to be a low priority indeed. There are more pressing health-care crises.

Certainly there is nothing inherently wrong with using drugs to enhance sexual performance, where the problem is far more frequently between the ears than below the belt. For millions of Americans, the ingestion of a couple of cocktails is as much a part of foreplay as the lingering kiss and the tender caress. The phenomenon is illustrated in the words of the English statesman who said he drank wine "to remove warts—from other people."

So, what's the problem with old Romeos taking Viagra and comporting themselves like young rams? Nothing, I suppose, if that's as far as it goes. But perhaps those people ought to pay for their own pleasures, and Viagra might end up to be one of those substances that create more problems than they solve.

Nevada brothels have reported a surge in business since the introduction of Viagra. Apparently, graybacks have been gobbling the stuff and reveling in their own randiness. This might not be such a bad thing in Nevada, where prostitution has been legalized and operates under strict hygienic regulations. In the other 49 states and the District of Columbia, it exists without such safeguards, and an increase in the trade could translate into an increase in AIDS, herpes, Chlamydia, gonorrhea and other wages of sin.

Even the most faithful husbands, pumped up by this stuff, can pose health risks. One little pill might be all that's required to get the dormant male machinery up and running, but how will Viagra affect the women? There have already been reports of vaginal bruising and tearing linked with Viagra, the result of ardent attempts to force, as it were, the rusty gate.

In the Los Angeles Times—that harbinger of things to come—an advertisement offers "vaginal rejuvenation" through laser surgery for women whose lovers have recently joined Team Viagra.

Putting gender bias aside, it does seem unfair that when a man pops a pill to rejuvenate his genitalia, a woman has to undergo surgery in order to accommodate him. Although there might be a benefit here for some women as well, I would not be surprised to see this inconsistency become a political issue. A group that dubbed itself Viragos Versus Viagra probably would not be lacking for charter subscribers.

Viagra might even affect religious doctrine. Perhaps it has already done so. You might have caught the news stories a couple of weeks ago about the

Southern Baptist Convention, whose board of governors recently approved a resolution calling for wives to "submit graciously" to their husbands. The telling phrase was cloaked and camouflaged by clauses and modifiers, but the decree came so close on the heels of the Viagra craze that it crowds the boundaries of probable coincidence.

Speaking of cause and effect, the Viagra phenomenon is itself only a symptom of a sickness that plagues American society: demographic bulge. It is surely no coincidence that as baby boomers enter the autumn of their years, science is suddenly discovering panaceas to dull or delay the ravages of time.

Besides the new hardness pill, there is also a new baldness pill. A giant pharmaceutical company not long ago introduced a little pill that purportedly can grow hair on a bowling ball. In some cases, alas, the baldness pill can have a deleterious effect on the sex drive.

Never fear! We have a pill for that.

Kaul, last of the liberals, inspired fledgling pundit

One of the most closely held beliefs of American conservatives is the myth of a liberal hammerlock on the nation's news media.

Oh, perhaps a few in the reportorial ranks have a pale greenish cast, but that's less a product of ideology than of the plethora of great environmental stories begging to be written. On the opinion pages, where political leanings are more evident, the conservative chorus sometimes threatens to drown out the few remaining liberal voices.

We're out of fashion and outnumbered, and our ranks are only getting thinner. Carl Rowan died last month, Molly Ivins is sick, and—worst of all—Donald Kaul has retired.

If you hate this column, blame Kaul. He was my inspiration.

Kaul recently wrote his last syndicated opinion. Maybe you saw it in the Tribune. It ended with a reiteration of his own columnist's creed: "You don't have to know what you're talking about to have an opinion."

I discovered Kaul when I was about 12. His column for the Des Moines Register, "Over the Coffee," was the thing that got me hooked on newspapers. He wrote mostly about Iowa subjects: the state legislature, girls' basketball, the bridges of Polk County. As Mike Royko was to the Windy City, Kaul was to the Tall Corn State.

As a teenager, I read all his columns and bought his books—"How to Light a Water Heater (and Other War Stories)" and "The End of the World as We Know It"—and unsuccessfully aped his style.

That style was unfailingly entertaining, mingling self-mockery and bemused skepticism. It had a little bit of Robert Benchley, a little I.F. Stone, a lot of Walter Mitty and a streak of Oscar Wilde. It could tickle, but it could also bite.

As a writer of opinions, Kaul went with his gut, and it rarely led him wrong. He hated cars and loved bicycles. He scorned television, and he despised the hollow culture of celebrity that has come to dominate the media agenda.

He was never afraid to voice an unpopular view. He called himself "Iowa's village atheist." I remember being a bit shocked when he deplored Will Rogers' famous statement, "I never met a man I didn't like," as false and pandering—which, when you think about it, it was.

Eventually, Kaul moved from Iowa to Washington, D.C., and his columns became more political and less personal. He also left the Register for a spell. As he tells it, "I got into a power struggle with an editor and was halfway through it before I realized I didn't have any power." That's a cautionary tale for columnists everywhere.

By the 1980s, the word "liberal" had undergone a pretty good working over. The neoconservative tide came in like the Galveston flood, and the new wave of right-wing commentators was determined to pigeonhole liberalism as the moral equivalent of pederasty. While other old-time lefties struggled to redefine themselves as "progressives" and "centrists," Kaul seemed to revel in the role of iconoclastic liberal in the age of Ronald Reagan.

Throughout the 1990s, he fired steadily away at his favorite targets—the National Rifle Association, the Christian Right, the Hollywood hit-making machinery—as upholders of violence and greed and purveyors of garbage. He wasn't always as funny as he was in the days when he wrote about Iowa girls' basketball, but he still dropped the occasional anvil on passing reactionaries, and he wielded a deadly needle that he used to deflate pompous gas bags such as Rush Limbaugh and Charlton Heston.

I expect Kaul has gotten more mail from the NRA than Brad Pitt has received from his millions of adoring fans. A different kind of mail it was, too, but Kaul seemed to like it. Everyone needs a love letter once in awhile, though, and this is mine to Donald Kaul.

The one opportunity I had to meet the man in person—when he spoke at my high school—I was too nervous to introduce myself. He'd probably laugh at that, but to me it would have been like meeting Mick Jagger or Bart Starr. I would have told him that I wanted to be just like him, and I have no doubt he would have urged me to aim higher.

I don't know. In retrospect, he set a pretty high standard.

Massage wasted on spa-resistant man

THERE ARE CERTAIN THINGS, LIKE MARXIST THEORY, TOE DANCING AND MALT liquor, for which a man must develop the taste while he is young or forever leave blame well alone.

Into that category I hereby consign all new age folderol. Probably one in three of my close friends clings to the belief that a pyramid, properly placed, is a holistic variant of Viagra. Nearly as many claim that a couple of crystals at the temples can shoo a migraine. And there is near unanimity among them about the therapeutic efficacy of saunas, body rubs and related spa activities.

Perhaps I was gulled by spectacular scenery and seductive company. How else to explain why, two short weeks ago, I found myself booked at an exotic spa whose exclusive offerings, if the brochure is to be believed, include getting one's face smeared with imported bird droppings.

Not that I went that far, although I'm sure nothing tones up the wattles like an application of guano. But I did follow the instructions and clad myself in a skimpy cotton kimono and a pair of plastic clogs. Descending icy wooden stairs, painfully wrenching my ankle along the way, I entered an office where I faced an efficient-looking young woman with a clipboard. She wanted my name, for no good reason that I could see. I suspected blackmail.

"Feliks, with a 'k'," I said, and she directed me to a waiting room crowded with slim young people, also in kimonos. I took a seat and tried to hide behind a home-decorating magazine until my alias was called. The first order of business was a scalding standard hot tub, alternated with icy plunges and followed by baking in a redwood sauna at 140 degrees for 15 minutes. This, it was said, would open my pores.

Once they had reached the size of manholes, I was hustled into a small room where a burly masseur beckoned me onto a table and thrust around me a blanket that had been soaking in a steaming vat of earthy-smelling soup. Thus was I introduced to the horrors of an herbal wrap.

"Relax," said my tormentor in a voice that brooked no opposition, and in a trice I was trussed up like King Tut, my elbows clamped to my ribcage, my legs immobilized and towels placed thoughtfully over my face to stifle my feeble cries. My heart was racing like a sewing machine, and my tongue felt like a bolt of flannel, but had I been able, I would have explained that my idea of relaxation entails a certain sprawling out and the clutching of a chilled beverage, preferably with a little umbrella in it.

Apparently, the concept of claustrophobia was unheard of in ancient Japanese society, from whence came the venerable tradition of the herbal wrap. And as any old Samurai warrior could tell you, there is an undeniable exhilaration that comes with the sensation of being buried alive. I can personally testify that it makes a measly half-an-hour feel like a geological epoch and greatly enhances one's appreciation of plain, ordinary fresh air.

After a month or so in the steaming, smelly blanket, my masseur unraveled me and got down to the real business at hand: the massage. "Relax," he said again, as though repetition would make it so. It didn't, although exhaustion and surrender must have provided a reasonable facsimile of relaxation, for he rolled me on my belly and with the deft touch of a piano mover proceeded to poke, pummel and prod me like a policeman searching the upholstery for a drug stash.

I had been told that the point of the massage was to empty one's mind of all earthly trivia and achieve a state of beingness, or maybe it was nothingness. Something along those lines. At any rate, I seemed quite unable to clear my brain of unhelpful cogitations, including the scandalous state of my toenails, the grating quality of the piped-in flute music and the fun I could have had spending my spa fee in a used bookstore.

About an eternity later, he rolled me over, sat me up and instructed me not to shower with hot water and soap for at least 24 hours because, he cautioned, the soap would clog my open pores. Being as he had just rubbed a half-gallon of perfumed axle grease into my tender white hide, I couldn't see how soap and water could do any real harm. But at that point, I was less concerned with argument than with escape.

He draped the kimono over my slumping shoulders and shunted me through a door and into the gift shop, where sales clerks tried to tempt me with polystyrene Buddhas, expensive unguents, erotic Asian art and bamboo-flute CDs. With a final mighty effort, I flung them aside and ran screaming into the night.

Well, I ended up coming down with the worst head cold of the millennium, not to mention a crick in the neck that froze me like Bartholomew Sholto in "The Sign of Four." I do not blame the spa—only my own rigid, typically Western inability to open myself to the ideas and experiences of the mystical East.

But from now on, I'm going to do my relaxing in a hot shower, with nothing but a cake of Ivory soap and maybe some banjo music. No bird droppings. I'd rather age gracefully.

Three-month-old Brennan captivates a proud papa in January 1990. "No matter how stirring your oration," wrote Forrest, "an infant will stare uncomprehendingly."

CHAPTER 4

DISPATCHES FROM THE HOME FRONT

Nightmarish memories of a Mennonite prom

ALL THE RESTAURANTS IN TOWN LAST WEEKEND WERE CRAMMED WITH HIGH school students dressed to the nines for that singular initiation into adulthood, the Prom.

The sight of so many rented tuxes and plunging bodices put me in mind of a true story. It is the saga of an incredibly handsome and talented youth who grew to sturdy manhood in a small city in Iowa. I was 17—for yes, I was that youth—in the acme of my acne and already beginning to date, when I met a girl who baby-sat for a family I knew.

Lucinda was the sort of girl your mom would call "very pleasant looking." She—Lucinda, not your mom—attended Iowa Mennonite School, about 12 miles down the road in a burg called Frytown. Apparently browned off on the Frytown bachelor set, Lucinda asked me to escort her to the IMS Senior Prom. I could hardly refuse.

When the big day came, I selected my dad's sportiest blue houndstooth polyester coat, white pleated slacks and blue suede platform shoes. To complete the rakish picture, I invested in a package of pastel-colored Egyptian cigarettes. I was determined to present to the farmers of Frytown a complete picture of a man-of-the-world.

I pulled into a dusty driveway heavy with the smell of hogs. Lucinda was resplendent in a daring gingham décolleté gown that flowed almost to her ankles. The fragrance of vanilla extract wafted from behind each ear.

When we reached the school, we were funneled with the rest of the student body into the gymnasium. Mennonites frown on dancing, so instead of hearing rock 'n' roll, we were seated in metal folding chairs specially chilled for the occasion and treated to a rendition of religious songs by the Heston Mennonite College choir.

An hour of lugubrious song was followed by dinner in the basement downstairs. As if my jaw were not sufficiently slackened and my eyes already glazed, the meal was preceded by a prayer easily as long as a full-blown Presbyterian sermon. We then sat down to a sumptuous Mennonite feast prepared by the students' mothers. Lime Jell-O with mayonnaise topping was followed by baked ham, mashed potatoes and green beans, with yellow cake for dessert.

Lucinda, in the meantime, had been casting lascivious glances and rubbing her ankle against mine so vigorously that it was beginning to chafe. I smelled trouble above the vanilla extract but threw caution to the winds.

Finally liberated from dinner, I suggested we drive to Iowa City where I knew of a hotel bar rumored to oblige pubescent prom-goers with cash on hand.

So enchanted was Lucinda with the dim lighting and other trappings of big-city sin that she drained a dozen daiquiris at $2.50 a throw. The management, spotting a couple of marks, didn't include a single drop of liquor in them, but Lucinda, inebriated by the heady atmosphere, proceeded to pinch me under the table till I could feel the bruises rising. The ash of an Egyptian cigarette melted a hole in my dad's jacket that I knew would be even harder to explain. With bankruptcy looming, I jingled the remaining pennies in my pocket and reminded her she had to get up and feed the chickens. She grumpily conceded.

As we pulled into the driveway on her father's farm, Lucinda seized the moment—and me. With arms made burly from years of lugging milk pails, she locked me in an iron grip and rained kisses on my perspiring face. Quickly, my coquettish squealing turned to screams of pure terror, but to no avail.

As I was about to pass out from the struggle and the odor of vanilla in a closed car, I heard salvation in the slam of a screen door.

"Cinda!" hollered a no-nonsense voice. "Get in here right now!"

"Mom ..." she protested, exiting the car with amazing agility for such a big girl. But I didn't wait around to see the rest. I was scratching gravel and driving home like a bat out of Frytown.

So much for my initiation into adulthood. It's been downhill ever since.

The most important rule in childbirth: Keep breathing

THERE'S A TRUE STORY ABOUT A WEARY FATHER OF FOUR STANDING OUTSIDE the hospital delivery room. After an interminable wait, a nurse appears and announces: "You have a beautiful, 8-pound son." To which he replies: "I'd rather have a beautiful, 8-pound bass."

That sort of macho stuff is no longer acceptable of the kinder, gentler male parent of the late '80s. As long ago as April, when I first found out I was to be a father, I vowed to take an active role in prenatal care and preparation up to and through the birth, when I can get back to watching the football game.

From the start, I've tried to assist my wife in little things like moving the refrigerator and making midnight runs to the ice cream store. As a former roommate to a premedical student, I had an impressive storehouse of misinformation I was eager to share. I knew already, for instance, that breathing was some sort of crucial element in childbirth. "Just keep breathing, honeybunch," I counseled. "Don't stop even for 10 minutes."

Unawed by my scientific knowledge, my wife defied the conventional and well-founded wisdom that old dogs are unteachable. She signed us both up for a six-week course on pregnancy, birth and early parenthood. As a caring and sensitive man, I, of course, was only too happy to attend. Who cares about an old pennant race, anyhow?

We found ourselves among 60 strangers in a room with dramatic fluorescent lighting above and linoleum underfoot. Although a dose of New Age elevator music nearly drove me out to check the baseball score on the car radio, I stuck with it.

A pleasant and sensible instructor ran us through a set of simple exercises and a generous catalog of useful information. She gave us telephone numbers to call and tips about diet, danger signs and other practical maters. She presently addressed the fathers in the class. Our role, she explained, would be that of "coach."

Having never played for a coach who struck me as caring or sensitive, I was initially bewildered. But I'm a by-the-book man, and I lost no time in cracking the manual: "Preparing for Parenthood." I studied the correct prenatal and postpartum procedures, paying special heed to the sections titled: "What the Coach Should Do."

"Your voice may be firm, but not harsh or strained," the manual told me. "Rest your hand gently on a tense muscle, or stroke it lightly, to help it relax." For example, "gently move the shoulders back and forth to note tension. Watch to see if the mouth, forehead and other facial muscles are relaxed."

"During practice sessions," it went on, "the coach should simulate contractions on the mother's body. To do this, apply firm pressure to some part of her body where it will apply discomfort. Apply pressure for 30-60 seconds." I combed the subsequent text for any reference to hobnailed boots and the cat-o'-nine-tails, but the manual was mysteriously silent.

When my wife arrived minutes later, I intoned the sadistic passage to her in a firm but soothing voice, noting with a professional eye the unmistakable increase in tension in her mouth and other facial muscles. Her shoulders rocked back and forth, and I had a fleeting fear that she was going to stroke her hand gently upside my head. But the lady in her triumphed over the tiger. "Just keep reading, smart guy," she said.

So, I'm reading and learning lots of helpful facts and interesting words. For instance, I always thought a kegel was a party, as in: "I heard the Delta Pi house is having a big kegel this Saturday." But the manual says pregnant women should do several hundred kegels every day, so I see now that I was confused. And now, if someone tells me, "Aah, your mother's a multip," I'll know he's only stating the obvious. Hoo-Ha Breathing, the Patterned Pant Blow and the Purf Routine are other sure-fire techniques that I have yet to master.

So, if you see me with my nose buried in a book, or my head resting lightly in my hands to help it relax, please don't say anything harsh or strained. With an 8-pound bass, I'd know just what to do. When it comes to 8-pound people, there's a whole lot more to know.

'The Sortin' Life,' or 'I've Got Plenty of Laundry'

On those rare occasions when I drop in at one of my old haunts, an acquaintance inevitably flutters down from the rafters and asks me where I've been hiding myself these days. I always answer best I can, but they're beginning to see through my stories about dangerous secret missions for the CIA's "Bibles to Libya" program.

Whenever I hazard the truth and tell them I've been staying home with my newborn son, Brennan, their response invariably is, "Oh, like 'Mr. Mom,' huh?" Actually, there's a lot more to it than that, as Barbara Bush could tell you. Those guys don't know what they're missing.

No doubt about it, the child-rearing life is the life for me. I'd just like to see somebody try to talk me into ruining my health with all-night revelry, dancing the Swamp Monkey with big-eyed floozies and drinking cheap champagne till my head spins. Yes, I sure would like to seem them try. I'll be waiting by the phone, in case anybody calls.

When I forsook my riotous youth to take up fatherhood full-time, I had pretty fuzzy notions of what child care was all about. After all, I thought, a baby sleeps most of the time anyway, waking only to coo softly until availed of a bottle. That done, I could get right back to tatting, tending my prize-winning rose bushes and writing my next best seller. Or so I believed.

Instead of bursting into the full flower of creativity, I have experienced a certain shrinking of perspective in the past six months.

The time I'd set aside to read the Harvard Classics is largely spent boiling bottles and sorting laundry. I find myself devoting the same sort of urgent attention to stool consistency that Keats did to the Grecian urn. When visitors call, I can't help but direct their attention to the cunning bears 'n' bunnies pattern on Brennan's nightwear—"jammies" is the technical term. And when his first tooth broke through last week, I broke into paroxysms of pride and had to be restrained from calling the wire services.

Now that my scion is beginning to move around on his own, I must maintain a constant vigil. The little tyke is showing an early knack for toppling floor lamps and mangling house plants. Like his father, he takes great pleasure in books, tearing the pages lovingly and chewing over every word. With the natural eye of the born connoisseur, he is fascinated by vases, fine crystal and costly breakables of all kinds.

The only thing that's missing is adult conversation. When I undertook this task, I swore to myself that I would never resort to baby talk, that I would address the youngster in complete and parsable sentences.

Little did I know that babies don't cotton to adult ideas of eloquence. No matter how stirring your oration, an infant will stare uncomprehendingly.

June 7, 1990

The moment you start making ape-man and airplane noises, their little faces light up and they start making sounds that, in your fevered imagination, could be "daddy."

And someday, it will be "daddy." That's the thing that keeps you going.

Dear Mom: Weather's fine, and brother is under arrest

You might think that words flow from my fingertips like the wine at an Italian wedding party, and it's true that I've churned out plenty of paragraphs in my career as a hard-hitting scandalmonger.

When it comes to the simple, joyous task of writing a letter to my mother, however, my mind takes on the consistency of a wrung sponge. Once I get past the weather and the health of her grandson, wild Arabian ponies couldn't drag a single noteworthy thought from my stymied brain.

In an attempt to summon the muse, I turned to a volume titled "Dearest Mother; Letters of Famous Sons to Their Mothers," published in 1942 by L.B. Fischer & Sons. What I found therein were not flawless, easily plagiarized pearls of prose but letters that not even a mother could love.

Among the first was a 1471 letter from Sir John Paston, an English knight, to his dear old mum.

"Moodre," it ran. "John Mylsent is ded, God have mercy on hys sowle! And Wylliam Mylsent is on life, and hys servants all be askepyed by all likelihood."

For all his noble qualities, Sir John apparently couldn't be troubled with a dictionary, and his scarcely literate jottings must have caused his mother much anguish.

George Washington avoided spelling altogether by abbreviating every word of more than two syllables. This simple device tended to give his filial devotion the tone of an invoice or a marching order: "You may acqt. Priscilla that her Son is very well, hav'g only rec'd a slight we'd in his Foot, w'ch will be cur'd with't detrimt to him."

Perhaps, I thought, military personages were ill-equipped to write thoughtful and engaging letters to their mothers. I leafed ahead to the correspondence of Wolfgang Amadeus Mozart, only to find that his letters lacked the mature style and graceful transitions of his musical works. I quote from one missive:

"I kiss Mamma's hand a thousand times! I too am still alive and, what is more, as merry as can be. I had a great desire today to ride on a donkey! I have a hard time, for in our rooms there is just one bed and so Mamma can well fancy that I get no sleep with Papa!"

Well! One could scour the annals of literature and not find a more perfect mingling of nonsense and disrespect.

Still, Mozart's childish scrawls are preferable to the letters of Napoleon Bonaparte to his mother. The emperor constantly implores her to intervene in sibling disputes, and all in all comes across as an unpleasant mixture of tinhorn tyrant and bossy brother.

"Jerome Bonaparte has arrived in Lisbon with the woman he is living with," Napoleon tattled in 1805. "I have ordered the prodigal son to travel by Toulouse and Turin and to report at Milan. I have told him if he varies this route, he will be arrested. ... I shall be inflexible, and his whole career ruined."

In a later letter, he whines about his brother Louis: "I taught him when he

___

was a child; I overwhelmed him with kindnesses. He repays me by libeling me
at every court in Europe. I appeal to you to spare me the pain of having to
arrest him as a rebel."

Old Mrs. Bonaparte probably threw up her hands and said: "Now Louis, you
be nice to Napoleon! And Napoleon, you quit arresting your brothers right this
instant, you hear?" What else is a mother to do?

Robert Schumann, the great German composer, obviously regarded his
mother as little more than a source of money and gifts. His letters have the
same ring as those of the callow freshman who sends his dirty laundry home to
be cleaned.

First, the buttering up: "Your every word is a living blossom." Next, the
casual acknowledgement: "I must also thank you for the check you sent me.
You would not believe how careless I am—I often actually throw money away!"
Finally, the touch: "I am curious to see what Christmas will bring. I much need
a new dressing gown, cigars, boots and a pair of stylish cuffs."

The letters of French novelist Honore de Balzac must have been a great
source of anxiety to his mother, because his main topic was his own lack of
robust health. "It is 11 at night and I am extremely ill from overwork," he wrote
her. "I have worked 160 hours on the book. I Have never been so tired, and you
will never know how much energy it cost to write you."

Eighteen years later, he was still alive and scribbling this cheery news:
"Since I wrote you last, I came down with such a frightful cold that I already
saw myself being buried here, having spat my lungs out." Yyych. Thanks for
dropping a line, son.

Obviously, there was little to be learned from the letters written by the good
and great, whose mothers saw them revealed as a passel of imbeciles, invalids
and ingrates.

Nothing remains but to forge ahead under my own feeble steam. So Mom, if
you're reading this, you should know that the weather is a little cooler and your
grandson is growing like a thistle. That's all for now, as I have an overwhelming
urge to go ride on a donkey. Y'r lvn'g son …

Some Christmas inspiration from a genuine living doll

'TIS THE TIME OF YEAR TO LIGHT THE OLD BRIAR, SPRAWL BACK IN YOUR COZIEST chair and watch your feet crackle cheerily on the hearth. There is no better setting for a comfortable evening spent thumbing through Christmas catalogs, the places where Santa Claus gets all his ideas.

Because the catalogs offer such a vast range of merchandise, it is wise to concentrate on a single area, such as power tools, stereo equipment or bathrobes. On one recent evening, I chose to explore the wide variety of dolls that toy makers are offering this year.

The most well-known figurines are Barbie and GI Joe. Incidentally, did you know that the sales of Barbie and Barbie accessories bring in about $600 million to Mattel every year? That's more than the U.S. government spends on the Food and Drug Administration.

At any rate, even though Barbie and Joe are firmly established as king and queen of toyland, they are not really dolls. The former is a fashion mannequin; the latter is promoted as an "action figure."

Far more interesting are the dolls that are trying to find a foothold on the market. The gimmickry far outstrips the mere walking, weeping and wetting dolls that have been around since my own childhood. Back then, Howdy Doody was a smash, Raggedy Annie was gamely holding her own and Barbie was just a brazen, busty upstart.

For sheer, stark realism, this year's dolls outdo them all.

There is one new product, a cuddlesome thing called Newborn Baby Shivers, that trembles alarmingly when its clothing is removed. The shaking, induced by a C battery, ceases as soon as Baby Shivers is clothed and hugged.

The Shivers child could be kin to Hush Little Baby, who cries out loud and incessantly until her keeper puts the specially designed bottle or pacifier in her mouth. Then, she stops crying and appears to suckle. Amazing.

Perhaps the closest thing to a real, live infant is a doll called Baby Uh-Oh. It not only wets, it actually develops a red rash on its little plastic bottom.

I have never pretended to understand what goes on inside the heads of little girls (or big ones, for that matter). But after more than a year of staying home to care for my infant son, I fail to see the allure of diaper rashes, cold shivers or constant crying. And the only good thing about wetting is that it signals the kidneys are still functioning.

However, if dolls that shiver, squall and break out in epidermal eruptions prove to be big hits, I must bow to the whims of the free market. In fact, I will embrace them. To prove it, I offer my 1-year-old son as a model for toy manufacturers who want to get in on the enfant terrible fad in time for next year's yuletide buying craze.

You might find these entries in the '91 Christmas catalogs:

Li'l Bruiser—An ingenious homing device lets this lovable doll toddle around unsteadily until he reaches the nearest hard, head-high corner, such as that on a typical table. As soon as he strikes it, L'il Bruiser lets out a scream like a wounded bear cub, which stops as soon as you take him for a ride in the car. But that's not all! Within minutes, a cunning, black-and-blue contusion appears at the point of impact, fading gradually into a yellowish discoloration that lasts for days, raising eyebrows in every supermarket checkout line. Takes four C batteries.

Baby Pukeums—This adorable doll picks up and eats small particles of all kinds wherever you leave them. Whether it's the bathroom trash can, the clothes hamper or any handy ashtray, Baby Pukeums will pluck out the inedible and put it in her mouth. When you try to remove the object with your finger, she will bite down with the strength of two mastodons. Moments later, she regurgitates an opaque fluid that is guaranteed to set your heart racing! Stomach pump not included.

Buster Babe—A devilishly clever doll, Buster Babe is outfitted with realistic, clutching hands that grasp and fling breakable objects. From a priceless Etruscan vase to the tiniest, irreplaceable glass miniature, Buster will search and destroy! Responds to cries of "No!" by turning momentarily and batting his lashes innocently before proceeding to the nearest hardwood floor and letting go. Also rips the pages from first editions.

You might think me a fool for freely giving away these million-dollar ideas, but let's just call it my contribution to the Christmas spirit. To add to the holiday ambience, I've also just loaded a large bundle of catalogs onto the grate, where they are now blazing merrily away.

It gives me a warm glow inside. So what if some toy manufacturer wants to make a fortune from a doll that is just like a real baby? I already have the prototype, and he's not for sale.

Profiles in cowardice, or Don't cross that line!

GENEALOGY BUFFS SHOULD HAVE THIS JOB. YOU WOULDN'T BELIEVE HOW MANY people write or call to tell me about my ancestry. The information takes many forms, most often with special emphasis on the maternal line.

But few do it as artfully as Tom Baumgardner, who sent me a couple of splendid documents relating to one of the Rose clan's most venerable members: Moses Rose.

The name brought back memories. I spent half my childhood in Dallas hearing about Moses Rose, aka Lewis Rose—the only deserter from the Alamo.

It would be hard to exaggerate the reverence for the Alamo in the Texas grade schools of my time, where state history was drilled into kids, and biology be damned. The heroes of the Alamo were demigods, Davy Crockett and Jim Bowie full-blown deities. Every family made a vacation to the San Antonio shrine.

By the fourth grade or so, I was heartily sick of Texas history. When the class did the annual Alamo catechism, bearing the family moniker became a heavy yoke for about a week. So thanks a lot, Tom, for bringing it up.

Actually, one of the documents is the best thing I've seen on the story of Moses Rose. It is titled: "Moses Rose's account of Travis Drawing the Line in the Dirt." It was submitted to the Texas Almanac in 1873 by members of the Zuber family, with whom Rose found shelter after he went over the wall.

According to the account, Alamo commander Col. William Travis gave a thoroughly rousing speech, replete with such passages as, "Our business is not to make a fruitless effort to save our lives, but to choose the manner of our deaths." And: "Let us kill them as they come! Kill them as they scale our wall! Kill them as they leap within! ... and continue to kill them as long as one of us shall remain alive."

I had to leave out a little carnage there to save space, but you can easily see that when it came to stirring speechifying, Travis made Knute Rockne look like Mortimer Snerd. Then Travis flashed his sword and drew the famous line in the dirt, inviting any and all to step across and die, gloriously, with him.

Naturally, being all heated up by the bloviating, they crossed it. The sick and wounded in their cots begged to be carried across the line and were obliged.

"Rose, too, was deeply affected but differently than his companions. He stood till every man but himself had crossed the line. He sank upon the ground, covered his face and yielded to his own reflections."

The report goes on to tell how Moses, who knew the local dialect, figured he could pass for Mexican and slip through the lines. He'd barely cleared the San Antonio city limits when "his ears were saluted by the thunder of bombardment, which was renewed. That thunder continued to remind him that his friends were true to their cause." Every defender died.

The other document is a pamphlet published by the Daughters of the Republic of Texas: "The story of the Alamo—Thirteen fateful days in 1836."

It adds little to Rose's account and neatly sidesteps the Moses-or-Lewis lebate by calling the sole deserter Lewis "Moses" Rose.

The Daughters' brochure does contain another item of interest. It lists the 189 who died fighting. Among them—I never knew this—was James Rose of Virginia. Great-great-great-great uncle Jimmy to me.

Actually, I don't know which Rose to claim. I'm awfully afraid my Rose elations would frown on the idea of accepting Moses Rose into the family circle. Not because he deserted the Alamo, but because he was French, and my branch has always claimed to be Scots-Irish.

Still and all, I won't deny Moses. If it hadn't been for him, there wouldn't have been an eyewitness account of the goings-on at the Alamo. There wouldn't be a legend. Every Texas schoolchild would never have heard about he line in the dirt and the patriots who, as the Daughters put it, "valued freedom more than life itself."

That wasn't grampa Moses. When he was interviewed as an old man in 1872, he was asked why he hadn't stayed behind. He replied, "By God, I wasn't ready to die!"

It's a line that will live down through the ages. It's a lot more inspiring than some corny phrase like "Remember the Alamo."

Columnist's father heroic in assassination aftermath

WHERE WAS I, 30 YEARS AND A DAY AGO? IN DALLAS, ENDURING ANOTHER DAY at Lake Highlands Elementary.

The memory is vague, just a roar of whispering, everyone hissing the same words: "Kennedy's dead!" When school let out early, my classmates and I did not, for the record, break into cheers. We slipped out silently, vaguely aware that an awful calamity had struck our nation and our city.

Years later, I found out my father, Earl Rose, was one of the few heroes in the tragedy that unfolded in Dallas that day. We children were not encouraged to discuss it outside the family, and to this day I hesitate to explore the subject with people I don't know and trust.

But after 30 years, the statute of limitations has run. Can I tell the whole world now? Dad, I'm so proud of you.

As Dallas County medical examiner, my father was required by law to perform an autopsy on anyone murdered within his jurisdiction. There were no exceptions for high federal officials—even presidents. So, when the Secret Service prepared to wheel John Kennedy's casket out of Parkland Hospital prematurely, he told them they couldn't do that until after he did an autopsy.

I can attest to something about my father's character: When he is sure of his ground, he is the Original Immovable Object.

For half an hour or so, he stood firm, unintimidated by threats and bluster. Finally, in a melee marked by shoving and shouting, the casket was removed, put on a plane and flown to Bethesda Naval Hospital.

The autopsy at Bethesda was performed under difficult circumstances, including a crowd of curious observers and a tight deadline. Without getting into the details, the doctors devoted more time than they should have, in retrospect, to cosmetic reconstruction and too little to forensic investigation. They did definitely establish two gunshot wounds that came from above and behind.

Despite those findings, the subpar post-mortem has proved to be the main wedge for Kennedy conspiracy theorists, who believe to a man that the autopsy was either faked or horribly botched. Many conspiracy buffs discount it entirely and draw up diagrams in which Dealey Plaza resembles the OK Corral.

No one can state flatly that if a proper autopsy had been performed in Dallas, there would have been no such controversies. This was, after all, the crime of the century. It is safe to say, however, that the questions would have been fewer, the suspicions less profound, the wild accusations more easily disproved.

Yep, Earl Rose is looking pretty sage right now.

It wasn't always that way, let me tell you. Several accounts of the confrontation—none flattering to my father—were published in the late '60s. He was depicted as a petty bureaucrat, throwing his puny weight around for the sake of a bit part on history's stage. He was called a die-hard states' rights dvocate—by implication a segregationist. He was described as belligerent, rrogant, cold-hearted.

I read these pieces and immediately flew into a red-eyed adolescent rage. low can they say this? This is completely unfair! For years, I would peruse hese scurrilities before every big basketball game because I knew they would vork me into an aggressive frenzy. It sounds silly, but it's true.

My parents wisely proscribed me from yakking about it. For one thing, I vas too far gone in the "My-pa-can-lick-yer-pa" mode. More important, they lidn't need the aggravation of all the neighbors asking questions and casting spersions.

Dallas, after the assassination, was beset with a paranoia that looks permanent and a wound that might heal but will never stop hurting. When we noved away 25 years ago, I swore I would never go back without an enormous inancial incentive. It's a vow I've had no trouble keeping.

By distancing ourselves from Dallas, the family was able to extricate itself rom the toils of the tragedy. But it was not until the mid-'70s that perceptions tarted to shift, that revisionists began seriously to question the conventional conclusions about the assassination.

In the past few years, interest in the case rose to near hysteria. My father was videly vindicated and praised. He was even depicted—for about two seconds y a 5-foot-tall actor—in the movie "JFK." Despite its historical and physical naccuracies, the scene tickled him greatly.

Still, he refused to grant interviews until late 1991, when he agreed to e questioned by a reporter from the Journal of the American Medical Association. The article, which appeared in May 1992, made him out to be a nan of great honesty and principle—perhaps the only person in Dallas that lay who was thinking clearly and acting forthrightly.

Well, that might be news to a lot of people, and I'm delighted to help spread t. But it's no news to me. I've known it all along.

Political slogans irrelevant to pursuit of real values

ON SUNDAY EVENING, A TIME I USUALLY DEVOTE EXCLUSIVELY TO PRAYER AND meditation, I wasted a full 90 minutes listening to the nervous yammering of the Kansas noncontender and the sugar-coated avowals of the Arkansas salve-spreader.

Subsequent hours were spent reviewing my copious notes, analyzing transcripts and dividing the viewership into the spin factor. I was about to affix my signature with a great flourish to a particularly penetrating column, when something intervened that seemed more relevant than the presidential debate.

My 6-year-old son and his pals had been thundering through, in, out and around the house while I worked. Presently, I wandered through the chaos and saw some items strewn around the floor. I picked them up and gently admonished my bairn to put things back where he found them.

"I didn't do it," he declared, and his friends echoed like a Greek chorus: "I didn't do it." My son—whom I knew to be the guilty party—glanced around to see who had already left the festivities. The he announced: "I think Jamie did it."

Later, when we were alone, I busted him. Lying to my face is unacceptable, I lectured him, and the fact that he'd falsely blamed an absent buddy was even more rotten.

"But Dad," he protested. "It was just a little white lie."

"No!" I was stern. "A white lie is a lie you tell to make someone feel good, like if you say, 'Dad, your hair looks good today.' What you did was just a plain old lie."

Lying was the one thing my father would spank me for. Choosing to spare the rod and unsure exactly how to proceed, I ordered him to sit by himself for 15 minutes and think of an appropriate punishment.

At the end of the proscribed period, I asked what he'd decided. Although chastened and subdued, he was inclined to be lenient. "I have to take a bath every night for two weeks, whether I yell or not," he said. Not enough, I responded. He would have to tell Jamie what happened and apologize to him—while I listened.

He cried a little. "I could kick myself," he snuffled. I felt the same and snuffled some, too. We hugged. We read "Attack of the Killer Pumpkins."

It wasn't long before Jamie showed up. I stood with folded arms and serious mien while my kid dolefully sketched out his treachery and concluded: "I'm sorry I lied and said you did it."

"That's OK," the other kid said. "I do that all the time." And away they went, laughing and shrieking, looking for new worlds to conquer, toads to torture and toys to demolish.

At that moment, it occurred to me that things like "trust" and "character" and "family values" are too complicated to be boiled down into simple slogans. Presidential debates notwithstanding.

Clumsy dad carves niche in finger, scouting history

As an astute student of National Geographic, I'm as familiar as any white man my size and weight with rites of passage as practiced by certain African and Australian native tribes. These rituals, gruesome to Western eyes, involve cutting thin strips of flesh from the grimacing initiate, then rubbing the wounds with some irritating compound to ensure scarification.

Amnesty International would be profoundly shocked to find out that right here in modern-day Mid-Missouri, fathers of young boys are required to undergo equally grueling ordeals. Granted, the scars I carry are mostly psychological. But I'll stake my last nickel—here it is, in my pocket—that they're as permanent and painfully acquired as those of any aborigine.

My son is a Tiger Scout, the first rung on the ladder of the Boy Scouts of America. Although I was never a Scout myself, it seemed to me that my 6-year-old son was old enough to start learning the traditional scouting skills: how to start a fire by rubbing two Bics together, how to smoke grapevine cigarettes, fundamentals of scatological humor and so forth.

As it turned out, the biggest feature of Tiger scouting is the annual Pinewood Derby, in which parent and son carve a miniature car from a kit consisting of a block of wood and four plastic wheels.

Many of the parents, especially the fathers, were eager to plunge into the project. These were the sort of men who own and operate lathes and band saws, belt-sanders and routers, who craft exquisitely detailed models of wooden sailing ships and make their own solid walnut dining room suites. I was not among them.

Nevertheless, I set to work with my pocketknife and wood chisel, whittling away at what appeared to be the front of the "car." Apparently, I had been issued a block of ironwood in lieu of pine, for I made slow headway. It briefly occurred to me that I might be using the wrong edge of the knife, but that mirage vanished when I slipped and brought the blade into contact with my index finger, which it sliced like a scalpel does cheese.

With Scout-like dispatch, I hastily improvised a bandage from toilet paper and Scotch tape—items readily available at any decently provisioned campsite. Then, aside from an occasional scream that rattled the windows, I bore the pain stoically and continued to carve.

I had envisioned a sleek minicar with modest fins—sort of a cross between a Lotus and an early Ford Fairlane. My son said it looked just like a prehistoric fish he'd learned about in school. To teach him manners, I made him sand out the chisel gouges.

Next, we had to deal with the matter of weight. Because gravity is the only accelerant in the race, the idea was to make the car as heavy as the rules allow: 5 ounces. There is reportedly a Web site devoted to the design and weight distribution of Pinewood Derby cars, and I suppose a proper dad would have downloaded this vital information. I just borrowed a decrepit postal scale from a riend, bored a hole in the block and inserted a couple of lead sinkers, filling in he rough spot with plastic wood, a marvelous substance that remains encrusted on the fingers for weeks.

My son did much of the painting and all of the critical decal and sticker work. I thought we were finished, but on race day, during the official weigh-in at he elementary school, our car was found to be almost an ounce under weight. ended up tacking four quarters to the bottom of the car. In the process, I reinjured my finger and had to be portaged to the nurse's station by eight Wolf Scouts.

In the school cafeteria before the race, the air was thick with either tension or macaroni and cheese. Scouts crowded excitedly around the wooden ramp-rack while the parents glowered competitively at one another.

The generous double-elimination format ensured that each car would race in at least two heats. Our car was eliminated after three heats, earning my son a seventh-place blue ribbon and securing my reputation for engineering ineptitude.

He seemed perfectly content, and who am I to complain? Maybe they'll even give me a badge.

Go ahead and pin it on my bare chest, like they do in the Marines. I've already endured tougher initiation rites than that.

How we spent our savings on summer vacation

EDITOR'S NOTE: FORREST ROSE IS RECUPERATING FROM PHYSICAL AND FINANCIAL exhaustion brought on by a two-week vacation. In lieu of his usual pasquinade, we are running a narrative by his traveling companion, edited only for spelling, libel and scrupulous accuracy.

Me and my dad went to South Dakota and it was mostly awesome except we had to drive across Nebraska to get there. Dad said it was the land of big skies but I think that means no trees or buildings or water slides. So I played Gameboy and read chapter books. I am 8. I am a good reader. I read mostly chapter books.

Dad kept stopping at all these museums even though he always complained they cost too much and the stuff wasn't that old anyway. It was pretty old, though. The old guns were cool. Our motel had a swimming pool.

After Nebraska, we went to Crazy Horse Mountain. He was a Sioux chief who beat Custer. He—my dad—said it was an outrage to charge $7 and still be three miles from the mountain when you can get almost as good of a view from the highway for nothing. He kept lifting up stuff in the gift shop and saying "Made in China" real loud so everyone looked, then had to spend like $100 or something in the gift shop so they wouldn't be mad.

Mount Rushmore was awesome. I can name the presidents. I am good at history. Dad liked it OK but his feet hurt, and he kept talking about the government parking monopoly and it being a crime to get nicked for $8, and that's what Thomas Jefferson wrote the Constitution about. He was one of the presidents—Thomas Jefferson.

Next, we went to the giant water-slide park that was awesome. My dad started coughing when they said $12 a ticket, and I was afraid we wouldn't go but he paid. I went on the Bonzai slide seven times. I'm a good slider. Dad doesn't like to be in public without a shirt but there were lots of people there just as white as him. Then we went to the giant maze that I liked but Dad said it was like being a steer led to slaughter and started getting real crabby till I found an emergency exit for him to get out.

The Badlands were the awesomest because you could climb around. I'm a good climber. Dad kept yelling to get back from the edge but I knew he wouldn't follow me out there. He's scared of heights. I'm a good climber, though.

He—my dad—said not to talk too much about the family reunion because people aren't interested in probate, whatever that is. But I did get to go swimming in the river and collect fossils. I'm a good swimmer. And once a rattlesnake rattled at me, and my uncle killed it and gave me the rattle because I was the one that made it rattle. I'm not suppose to tell Mom but she doesn't read his articles so it's OK. I know a lot about venomous animals.

I also got to drive a team of horses for a whole mile. I was really good at driving the wagon. When we got home, Dad said I should just as well have driven us home in the wagon for all the road construction detours and delays, but wasn't it a great vacation?

South Dakota is a very big state with hardly any trees or vegetables but has some really awesome things too like Badlands and rattlesnakes. I know a lot about South Dakota.

Photos can document fashion faux pas

LET ME ACKNOWLEDGE RIGHT FROM THE START THAT I HAVE THE FASHION SENSE of a mackerel—and not a very spiffy mackerel, at that. If I can match the socks and get the underwear label around to the back, I figure I'm already ahead of the game. It has ever been thus.

These days, I've also been buying clothes for my 9-year-old son. He'd been wearing his jeans without a belt so that they sagged sadly on his scrawny frame. Although he had to hold up his pants with one hand—a definite handicap at recess—he was determined to maintain the baggy look considered stylish by discriminating Columbia third-graders. So, I bought him a pair of baggy-cut jeans that would stay up but still have the proper "gangsta" look.

Well, quicker than you could say "Oshkosh B'Gosh," an attractive young matron—his mother, actually—was questioning my judgment. To her, the jeans represented a misogynistic, violent culture, and she didn't want our son to imitate it or associate with it in any way.

You might already have heard the history of this particular fashion. The baggy jeans fad followed the first wave of prison construction in the 1980s. Prisoners were stripped of their belts so that their pants drooped down around their hips. The look was adopted by the 50 percent or so of young black men on the street, along with the backward ball cap. Anyway, I doubt our son or his peers are familiar with these antecedents, seeing that they took place before he was born.

There's also the fact that specially-cut "gangsta" pants are commonly available—on the sale rack, yet—at places like J.C. Penney and Kmart. What was once a statement of rebellion has been gobbled up in the consumerist maw: masticated, digested and leached of all rage and radicalism so it can be marketed to the masses.

Baggy jeans have gone from trendy to popular and finally to passe. In that regard, they are like all fashions. Take the turtleneck. In the 1950s, it was worn primarily by disreputable beatnik types as a protest against button-down shirts and button-down minds. Who wears turtlenecks today? Mostly corporate executives striving for a casual look at the cocktail hour. Of course, they could be hip again and I just haven't heard about it.

In any case, baggy jeans stopped being a ghetto-chic thing the second 9-year-old suburban white boys started wearing them. And in a couple of years, maybe less, they'll all be wearing bell bottoms, which appear to be in vogue on campus these days.

I never went for bell bottoms myself, although they were the apex of style when I was in high school. I wore roomy, ragged work jeans with a hammer loop on the leg. Preferred brand: Big Smith. My dad would mutter something about pants that looked like a whole family of Calcutta beggars just moved out of 'em. Mother just hoped the people who saw me knew I did my own clothes shopping. I didn't care. With my spacious denim trousers, high-top Converse All Stars and longish hair, I thought I looked pretty cool.

It's painful now to view those 25-year-old Polaroids. What I see is a big-toothed boy with the normal quota of adolescent complexion problems, disheveled hair, a neck like a swan and jeans that appear to have been handed down from Jackie Gleason.

Every upcoming generation considers it a positive duty to cultivate a style that shocks and dismays the preceding generation. When my son reaches that phase, for all I know, he might be wearing eyeliner and ballet shoes just to get a rise out of the old man.

But I'm ready for him. I've got the camera loaded, and in time that will be punishment enough.

Fashion is fickle. Vanity lasts forever.

All balled up by Christmas conflicts

Pull your chair up here, laddie, close to the sun lamp, and let's have a straight talk about the true meaning of Christmas.

There must be people who aren't torn about the holiday and all it has come to signify. They are actually invigorated by mobs of shoving shoppers. They delight in Dennis Rodman's X-treme Xmas Wrestlerama and still laugh hysterically at the barking version of "Jingle Bells." There are, in fact, many millions of such people.

Then, there are the rest of us, for whom the holiday period invariably takes a heavy toll on the soul. It can't be just the long nights, the raw chill of winter and the inevitable spate of bad new movies. No, 'tis the season itself.

How can a thinking person not be conflicted about Christmas? Christmas itself is conflicted almost beyond redemption.

We all abhor the crass commercialization of Christmas, or at least we affect abhorrence. This is a holiday to celebrate the birth of Jesus of Nazareth, who later in life laid extremely poor odds on the chances of rich people ever getting to heaven. He also gained considerable notoriety when he chased the moneychangers out of the holy temple.

You don't have to be a writer for Leno to get the irony: In the subsequent millennia, the birthday of Jesus has morphed into something beyond the moneychangers' wildest dreams of avarice. The day heralds an annual orgy of buying and selling, shameless hucksterism and slavish consumption. Santa Claus is really nothing more than Mammon in red pajamas.

This I believe. So, I look with some dismay on all the presents I purchased this weekend: a lamp with moving cartoon fish and another with cartoon stars and planets; a cheap necklace modeled on a string of tiny Christmas lights; a pocket-tool kit in a handsome wood-grain carrying case; a plastic dancing hula girl; scented novelty candles; a leather fly swatter. In short, as big a load of useless garbage as ever got hauled out on a scow—or in on a sleigh.

The preceding list is only fragmentary, a partial catalog of obligatory purchases for out-of-town relations who are highly unlikely to read this column before Christmas, which of course would spoil the suspense. There is more— much, much more—that I cannot list. Any honest accounting of the full inventory would embarrass a Byzantium emperor.

My siblings and I have made feeble attempts over the years to cut down our gift-buying to a reasonable level. There have been proposals to draw names, to place a dollar limit on purchases, to exchange homemade gifts. Always, there were objections from one quarter or another or demands that exceptions be made—"No limit on gifts for the kids!" Whatever arrangements we tentatively agreed upon always crumbled, as tends to happen in any voluntary cartel.

Privately, over a glass of grog, many of us will admit to our frustration and seeming hypocrisy. But we buy into the scene year after year. The reason, I believe, is a powerful sense of obligation. So pervasive is the pressure to exchange gifts, so ingrained are the expectations that a renunciation of the tradition would be nothing short of drastic.

Want to alienate your friends and family and get your acquaintances whispering about you behind their hands? Tell them nicely but firmly that you will no longer give or accept Christmas presents. Then, follow through. When your Uncle Ben or Aunt Bunnie sends you that beanbag massager or shoe tree you've been wanting, send it back with a polite no-thanks.

"Scrooge" will be the nicest thing they call you.

There are Christmas traditions that even the worst Scrooges among us can enjoy. There's the ritual cutting down of the Christmas tree, followed by the ceremonial trip to the emergency room to repair the ugly gash on your hand. There's the unforgettable look on a child's face when he opens up the Sega game you've given him when what he wanted was Nintendo.

Happy holidays. And turn up that sun lamp.

Forrest takes a break from his Sunday morning radio show at KOPN in the early 1980s.

CHAPTER 5

ABOUT TOWN

City pot-arrest crackdown needs healthy public debate

TRUTH IS I LIKE MY LOVE MAIL—BUT I LIVE FOR THE OTHER KIND. DON'T GET ME wrong, I appreciate it when Tribune readers agree with what I've written. It's just that I'd rather have a good argument than eat pie.

On last Tuesday's Opinion page, Columbia police Capt. Tom Dresner gave me all the argument I could ever hope for. He said I "crossed the line" the week before when I chided the department for cracking down on nonviolent possessors of small amounts of marijuana.

Columbia police used to direct nearly half of such cases to municipal court. Under chief Norm Botsford, they now submit almost all of them to state authorities. The practical result of the policy is that the arrested person must pay a bail bondsman or spend the night in jail, and a state conviction means a permanent criminal record.

This is a legitimate public-policy issue, and it needs to be publicly discussed. It's a pity that fear of unfair insinuations has made many people hesitant to speak out. On the other hand, Darwin Hindman, Ann Landers and William F. Buckley Jr., among others, are already on record as opposing harsher measures for pot smokers. I like that company.

Columbians obviously feel strongly about the issue. One caller accused Capt. Dresner of employing intimidation tactics to silence criticism, while a letter-writer instructed me to be ashamed of my forgiving attitude on marijuana. And there is much, much more.

Granted, both Dresner and I write provocative prose, but after a long and cordial telephone conversation with him last weekend, I can report that neither one of us is the menace our worst detractors make us out to be.

I must confess the captain caught me out on a couple of points. Botsford didn't create a special drug enforcement unit, as I said he did. He just doubled the size of the existing unit. And Dresner informed me that handcuffing is not reserved exclusively for state cases. A Columbia officer may clap the bracelets on someone receiving a municipal summons and detain the suspect at police headquarters.

He also made me aware of a glaring omission in my column, to wit: The Columbia Police Department is, by and large, an exceptionally professional outfit. In my personal dealings with Columbia police, they have been competent and courteous. I should have said that.

At the same time, I was able to wring a couple of small concessions from this loyal and strong-minded police captain. For one thing, he acknowledged the difference between pot and harder drugs like heroin, meth and cocaine. Marijuana is far milder in effect, and less destructive and addictive, than those narcotics.

This is a key distinction, and the Columbia City Council granted it legislative recognition in 1984. The city ordinance gives police flexibility; the current "philosophy" ensures a rigid police response to every arrest for simple possession.

Dresner was especially riled that I had equated Botsford's approach to "letting people know they've been bothered." Believe me, I would've liked to take those words back, but I couldn't because they weren't my words. They were uttered by a Columbia police officer in reference to the new pot arrest policy.

There is also the question of whether the crackdown constitutes a wise and efficient use of public resources. From his own patrol experience, Dresner knows it takes more time and effort to haul an alleged doper out to the jail in Prathersville than it takes to write a summons, or even to take the suspect downtown.

By the same token, it strains credibility when officials at the Boone County Jail say the 300-plus people brought in on minor pot charges last year didn't pose any significant additional burden. These same officials have lately been complaining loudly about jail overcrowding, doubtless preparing the public for another tax increase.

Well, not everybody jailed for simple pot possession bonds out right away. Some of them have to stay in jail overnight until the next day's arraignments. The rest have to hang around to be booked and wait for bail. How many deputy-hours and how much jail space do they all occupy in the course of a year? If the crowding crunch is half as bad as the authorities say it is, any additional burden ought to qualify as significant, especially if it can be avoided.

Neither Dresner nor I knew how many misdemeanor pot suspects made bail and how many didn't. In fact, we found a vast common ground in the things we didn't know. We didn't know how often state charges are dropped, or how often a guilty plea results in a suspended imposition of sentence. We weren't sure whether the racial breakdown of pot possession busts accurately reflects the city's racial makeup. We had no idea whether the city council or the city manager can give the police chief a directive or even a recommendation in this matter.

So, there is still plenty of room for people smarter than us to join in this debate. Although I was unable to change Dresner's mind, it remains my completely objective opinion that I am right and he is wrong. But reasonable people can disagree, and that's a fact.

A number of people have asked me whether the Trib Talk line has caller ID. I have been informed that it does not. The number is 815-1776.

Rowdy fraternity parties belong back in Greektown

WHEN YOU'RE TRYING TO FIND THE PULSE OF THE TOWN, IT'S SOMETIMES HARD TO KNOW whether what you're feeling is really just the throb of your own preconceptions.

So I was glad to see my esteemed publisher, Hank Waters, make some incisive observations about the off-campus activities of MU Greeks. "They make the march of the Visigoths look like an Easter parade," he wrote.

This alarming image was based on reports about MU fraternity parties held at remote locations, particularly one recent bash at Easley, on the Missouri River. Thousands gathered at the lovely site, and as the hours wore on and the party waned, there were too few buses to transport the partygoers back to Columbia.

Some stranded party guests stole bicycles and tried to ride them back to Columbia. More than one motorist on the River Road found his vehicle surrounded by drunken revelers, rocking the car and demanding a lift. It had to be an unnerving experience, like trying to get out of Saigon in '74.

Some folks had their cars shelled with rocks and bottles. One besieged couple called the Boone County Sheriff's Department, which administered the salt-rub. As the squad car came screeching up, the citizen mistook it for another assault and dinged it with a stool. The sheriff demands that he pay for the damage.

Another fraternity made an excursion to Octoberfest and got out of hand at a Hermann winery. According to a report in The Maneater student newspaper, the fellas apparently overturned some tables, stole some floral display carts and generally behaved with maximum obnoxiousness. Later, the house wrote a letter of apology that was published in the Hermann newspaper, and the winery owner declined to press charges.

That letter was about the closest thing any Greek house has shown to taking responsibility. The president of the fraternity that trashed the winery refused to comment on the incident, The Maneater said. In fact, no one in the house could comment because they were all said to be in mourning for the late golfer Payne Stewart. I sure am glad they have their priorities straight.

As for the Easley riot, leaders of the fraternity that threw the party said it couldn't possibly be held to blame for the misbehavior of unidentifiable guests. As Hank put it, they are "resisting pressure to make amends for vandalism done by unknown individuals." MU officials agree the frat house shouldn't be held accountable.

I'm not so sure. If your neighbor has a big party and some guest tramples your flower bed or scrapes your car, shouldn't the host bear a little bit of the responsibility for the damage to your property? The only person at Easley who's being forced to cop to anything is the trapped motorist who accidentally dented the police car. That's just wrong.

At the very least, the sponsoring fraternity failed to arrange for adequate transportation back to campus. The lingering hordes were left to prey on the local population. The host frat ought to have kept at least one brother sober enough to supervise the buses and make sure some of them stayed late enough to ferry the stragglers.

Although it hurts, I have to part company with Hank when he says the University of Missouri should stick with its policy of keeping alcohol off campus.

About 10 years ago, a high school kid climbed a utility pole and got himself electrocuted and damn near killed at the infamous "Bid Day Bash," a Greektown street party. The rowdy crowd refused to part for the arriving ambulances.

Horrified MU officials banned "keggers" on campus, and frats began moving their orgies elsewhere. The reaction was understandable. The problem is the result. "Dry campus" sounds good, but it doesn't work out so well in practice.

Instead of staggering safely back to their own nearby houses, Greek partygoers now must drive to and from the parties—or find someone who will. Don't try to tell me the "dry campus" policy doesn't put more drunken drivers on the road, because simple logic tells me it does. When no drivers are available, you get debacles like the one at Easley.

Because the old-fashioned frat house "keggers" are banned, students at the off-campus parties usually have to bring their own liquor, and that hasn't exactly cut down on drunkenness. It has, however, increased the amount of broken glass and other garbage.

There is something to be said for keeping Greek parties in Greektown. They have the facilities for it, goodness knows. If you've ever been in any of the bigger houses, you can see they are especially designed for drunken revelry.

If the streets of Greektown are clogged by celebrants, it's an easy thing for a motorist to go around, an option that doesn't exist in, say, Easley. If the beer hogs in attendance commence to thieving and destroying property, at least their ruffian behavior will be directed at their own kind, not inflicted upon the rest of the citizenry.

For that matter, it would be a whole lot easier to police the mob in Greektown, where there are two separate police forces within shrieking distance. The undermanned sheriff's department, which has to patrol far more territory with far fewer resources, can barely spare a single deputy to respond to such calls.

The way in which the Greeks comport themselves is important to all of us. I call your attention to the current Time magazine college guide. Its one-paragraph summation of MU contains the sentence: "Greek life is big." For many townies, it's kind of like living by the stockyards: It stinks, but you get used to it.

Against this backdrop, consider the reaction of many Greeks to the recent attempts to buy a vacant frat house, which would be used as a residential facility for recovering alcoholics.

One sorority member summed it up when she told the Tribune: "I can't believe they're even, like, contemplating that."

Like, wow, it must be a scary prospect, having a bunch of creepy old drunks hanging around the neighborhood instead of only the creepy young drunks she's accustomed to.

Relatively few undergraduates have extensive experience with recovering alcoholics. Speaking as one who has, I have found there is no one more sober—or somber—than a typical 12-stepper. They tend to dourness. Such a halfway house in the midst of Greektown could well serve as a valuable cautionary lesson to the surrounding residents.

They need some lessons. The entire idea of "community service," as embraced by many fraternities and sororities, seems to consist of skipping rope or some other silly stunt in behalf of the Jerry Lewis telethon. They need to wake up to the fact that it also means being part of the community instead of excluding it and caring for the community instead of trashing it.

Mommy, what's that bronze man doing?

WITH THE FULL COOPERATION OF THE WEATHER, FOR ONCE, ART IN THE PARK was a gorgeous success this year, allowing many of the best artists in the area the opportunity to showcase their considerable talents.

With all the gifted artists we have around here, it's a puzzlement how much of our public statuary is so consistently second-rate. Take, for example, the cute little instrument-playin' critters on the Boone County Courthouse lawn, a piece so utterly fey it would make Mister Rogers retch.

Now, it has been surpassed by a new artistic display with far more serious pretensions. I refer to the hodgepodge at First National Bank, downtown at Broadway and Eighth Street, that has moved out of its pocket-park niche and threatens to engulf the sidewalk.

The most striking aspects of the First National artworks are their obvious costliness and their thrown-together quality. It's as though some mad art collector had decided to put on a triple retrospective, a show featuring the works of Norman Rockwell, Andy Warhol and Jackson Pollack. Great 20th century artists every one, their paintings were never meant to hang alongside one another. To do so would diminish them all.

The centerpiece of the First National space is a giant sculpture that I will attempt to describe, although believe me, you really need to see it for yourself. It's hard to miss.

A stone-and-tile pedestal supports the sculpture itself. Upon the pedestal rest three identical kneeling bare-breasted bronze women, all of them wearing what look like the helmets of the Deaths' Head Hussars. On their shoulders they hold up a sort of cylindrical thing made of metal bars, which in turn supports the iron lineaments of a globe. I think it's supposed to be the world. It could be a hot-air balloon. But naked women wouldn't have to hold up a hot-air balloon, so I think it must be the world. Atop the sphere, a triangular blue tile flag is frozen in mid-flap.

Five equally naked bronze men are striking various attitudes all over the globe. The guy right in front, with a full beard and Michelangelo muscles, has his arms outstretched in the classic crucifixion posture, except his palms are down in the style of a diver about to propel himself from the end of the board. Another man sits just above him, facing the opposite way and looking for all the world like he's about to defecate on the first fellow's head. Sorry to be vulgar, but hey, I didn't make the statue. A third man is doing a Frankenstein walk; a fourth seems to be jumping. The fifth is striking the Heisman Trophy pose, except he's toting a bronze pigeon instead of a football.

Bronze birds are distributed all around the First National art space, a feature that does have some recognizable symbolism. In the old days, real feather pigeons would have provided a unifying theme, depositing their leavings on sculpture good and bad in the time-honored way. The city long ago poisoned the live pigeons downtown, but now we have much more sanitary metal ones to console us.

This sculpture definitely stands on its own, although about 10 determined art lovers with a grappling hook could probably change that.

It dominates the upper stratum of the space, but ground level belongs to the massive tile-and-stone benches. They are huge hulks with sweeping curves and California-colorful mosaic motifs. In a real park with trees, grass and room, they would be splendid. Unfortunately, the nearest grass is two blocks away at the Veterans Memorial, and they probably wouldn't go so well there, either.

But in front of the bank, with its straight lines, brown brick and mirrored windows, the effect is weirdly like that of Groucho glasses on a Lutheran minister. It almost overpowers the benches' dissonance with the Rodin-esque globe sculpture. Almost.

The benches do have the notable virtue of providing places to sit. Their seating capacity, however, is not commensurate with their great size, and when two of these whales showed up on the sidewalk recently, all right-thinking people were outraged.

I mean, they're blocking half the walkway, and they have the look of permanent fixtures. I didn't know the city allowed private businesses downtown to do that. All I do know is that I don't like being jostled when I'm walking around, and I am holding the directors of the bank strictly accountable for any violations of my personal space.

My favorite piece of art at the bank is an iron fence skillfully wrought to resemble grasses and grains. It's a spectacular work, satisfying to gaze upon despite the clashing background.

Clearly, whoever picked out most of these pieces has excellent taste. And whoever decided to put 'em all together obviously suffered a regrettable lapse. When you have a lot of art in a little space, it appears possible to over-celebrate diversity.

Twenty years later, kids, this Note's for you

GATHER 'ROUND, CHILDREN. STAY VERY STILL AND KEEP YOUR HANDS IN EACH other's laps, and Grandpa will tell you all about the old days in Columbia, when computers were the size of refrigerators, there were no kiosks downtown and no such nightclub as The Blue Note.

It was about 1980. I was making upwards of $80 a week in the music business, working the circuit from Junction City, Kan., to Bettendorf, Iowa, and existing between gigs in the slums of East Campus.

My two neighbors, Phil Costello and Richard King, made camp in a hovel even more leaky and roach-ridden than my own. They were itinerant carpenters who spent their nights mixing Singapore slings and sloe-gin fizzes in such long-forgotten nightspots as Fannie Keenan's and Fish & Friends.

One afternoon, I was quietly loitering in a local billiards establishment when Rich and Phil came in, looking as if they'd just gotten done with a particularly rough roofing job. Phil, a conspiratorial look on his face, broke the big news in a stage whisper that could shatter glass: "Frost, I think we're gonna buy the Brief Encounter."

The Brief Encounter, a cavernous bar on Business Loop 70, was frequented by a handful of Harley-Davidson enthusiasts and hardly anybody else. It wasn't what you'd call a fancy joint, but I still didn't see how these two ne'er-do-wells would be able to swing it.

True, they knew a lot about music. They'd told me about this guy, Elvis Costello, who was the hottest new thing. The Dead Kennedys, the Ramones, the Blasters. We had intense conversations about meaningless topics: Does Bruce Springsteen ever have an off night? Richard: "Never!" Me: "Everybody does."

Through a combination of bluff and blandishment, Richard and Phil had managed to pry a loan out of some gullible citizen, and they were determined to make it happen. Then, for the first and last time, they asked for my advice.

"Lots of posters," I replied. "Posters are the cheapest, most effective advertising you can get. Plaster every telephone pole and bulletin board."

Looking back, I'd like to think that in my small way I was indirectly responsible for the passing of a municipal littering ordinance, not to mention numerous shouting and shoving matches.

Well, The Blue Note was a hit from Day One. Phil, who embodied the term "smart aleck" and dressed like a pimp on a golfing vacation, was the front man who booked the bands. Richard, the more mild and reasonable partner—oh, you think I'm lying?—handled the bar and hired the personnel.

And what personnel! I'd have to say we were about as merry a crew as you could find for $4 an hour apiece. I secured myself a post as doorman, which really didn't involve much more than collecting the cover charge. In those far gone days, management frowned upon checking IDs. It was considered bad for business.

The hardest part of my job was keeping out interlopers from the Pow-Wow Lounge, a rough bar right next door. Every once in a while, some seedy old redneck would stumble into The Blue Note, where I would greet him with a cheery: "That'll be $15, please." I endured some pretty impressive cussings in those days—even more than now.

The music made it all worthwhile. In those days, The Blue Note specialized in booking national acts on the way up or down. We heard Ricky Skaggs, then trying to break into the mainstream country market. The legendary Sam & Dave brought in their soul combo and put on one of the best shows I've ever seen anywhere. The bluegrass stalwarts Hot Rize came through, as did Black Flag, Taj Mahal, Maria Muldaur, Chubby Checker and countless others I was too inebriated to remember. Koko "Queen of the Blues" Taylor was still near the height of her powers and made The Blue Note one of her regular stops.

Naturally, the club booked local and regional acts as well. Among them was Fool's Face, a bunch of talented and pretty fellows from Springfield who attracted a monster following, and an art band from Kansas City called DuChamp, which featured a fabulously androgynous lead singer.

A few years later, Phil moved to Chicago and then to Los Angeles, where he became a successful record company executive and dropped out of sight. I'm told he's quit shaving, wears Kleenex boxes on his feet and has developed a phobia of country and western music. He was leaning that way already, though.

A good many people didn't think Richard would be able to keep the enterprise afloat, but he displayed the grit and business acumen that has made his name a word. The Blue Note moved downtown, into the old Varsity Theater location. Richard quickly discovered that young people would pay for the privilege of dancing to records, and lo, the weekly dance party was born.

I don't get down to The Blue Note as much as I used to. Oh, every once in a while, I'll dodder on down to catch Leo Kottke, Steve Earle or some other relic, but the general run of the clientele makes me feel like the original Grayback from Wayback.

I wouldn't say my rocking days are over. It's just that now, I've got a special chair for that.

Deposit law unmourned — for now

THERE ARE TWO SCHOOLS OF THOUGHT ABOUT A MONUMENT TO THE DEAR departed beverage container deposit ordinance. Many believe it deserves something the approximate size and shape of the Great Pyramid of Khufu, made entirely of discarded cans and bottles and already under construction at the local landfill. Others favor a more tasteful emblem—a smattering of red, white and blue cylinders against a field of green. Unfortunately, it looks as though we might get both.

Was anyone really surprised that the fourth attempt to repeal the ordinance was successful? Deposit supporters seemed worn out by repeated battles, unable to muster the enthusiasm of past campaigns.

I knew in my heart the deposit law was doomed when, a week or so before the election, some kooky old lady was caught pilfering pro-repeal campaign signs. That boneheaded maneuver seemed to convey, in a cartoonish and pathetic way, the quiet desperation of deposit supporters. "If every one of us could just pull up one blue repeal sign, we might have a chance."

Any astonishment at the result should have been eliminated with the subsequent release of campaign finance disclosure reports. It turned out the repeal forces spent $88,000 plus change to get about 10,000 votes. That is a staggering sum. I doubt anyone has ever spent even one-fourth as much on a municipal April election.

My math isn't what it used to be—in fact, it never was—but I think $88,000 would have paid the nickel deposit on 1,760,000 cans and bottles. It also works out to about $8.80 per pro-repeal voter, a sum that equals the nickel deposit on 176 cans or bottles.

Based on those calculations, I hereby offer my short-term plan for a Neat & Tidy Columbia. Every person who voted for repeal is obligated to pick up 176 beer and soda cans or bottles littering the landscape. I'm not talking about their own cans and bottles or the ones they could easily collect at the office or the country club. I mean fishing out the ones down there in the gully or in the trash bins downtown—the ones homeless people used to pick up—and putting them in the blue recycling bags. Do your part, Fred Parry!

Fred and his pro-repeal brethren repeatedly preached during the campaign that the public-spirited citizenry of Columbia would keep the city streets litter-free even without the extra nudge of a nickel deposit. My plan calls on them to demonstrate their own commitment to that worthy goal. I realize it's only a stopgap, but it might help tide things over until the Columbia City Council gets off the stick.

That could take a while. Less than a week before the election, five members of the council publicly said they thought the deposit law was fixable. This backhanded endorsement was particularly puzzling considering that the ordinance, which had some obvious flaws, was never amended despite a city task-force study that lasted almost two years. If they thought it was fixable, why in blazes didn't they fix it?

With the repeal, any financial incentive to recycle has been removed. Our business community leaders, who profess to believe in the power of the market, perversely refuse to acknowledge that the nickel-a-can deposit was a primary motivating factor in keeping solid waste not just out of the landscape but also out of the landfill.

Restoration of some sort of financial inducement could greatly assist recycling efforts. The most obvious would be a pay-as-you-throw approach to municipal garbage pickup. Under the current system, everybody pays the same high monthly rate of $10.75 no matter how many black bags they leave on the curb and no matter what's in them. This is a big bargain for the people who generate a lot of solid waste and a big gyp for the people who don't.

A system that charges according to the amount of solid waste makes sense, although it is vulnerable to cheating. If the price is too high, many a skinflint will start leaving his garbage bags at somebody else's curbside, furtively disposing of it in institutional Dumpsters or even just tossing it in a ditch. Some folks might even put their nonrecyclable trash in blue recycling bags just to avoid the charge. Nevertheless, other cities have implemented such plans with success, and the pay-as-you-throw system would at least restore some semblance of rationality to our municipal solid-waste management.

We'll also need to expand the blue-bag recycling program, which does not now serve many thousands of apartment dwellers in Columbia. There also will have to be a lot more drop-off places for recyclables. Perhaps some of our more civic-minded purveyors of beer and soda can set aside some parking spaces for the necessary bins.

In the meantime, those messy monuments are getting bigger every day. If we don't take action soon, the landfill will run out of room and the landscape will be despoiled. On that dark day, no one should be astonished to see a streamlined, amended deposit ordinance make it back to the ballot. Because, flawed as it was, it worked.

30-foot sticker could save 'Tiger Spot'

WITH MALICE TOWARD NONE AND CHARITY TO ALL, I OPENED MY SUNDAY Tribune to read an article about the recent travails of Paul Jackson, Columbia's most commercially successful artist.

It has been "a rough year" for Jackson, the article reported. His downtown gallery, Illumia, will close next month. His design for the tail-side of the Missouri quarter was altered against his wishes. With his imminent divorce, he will lose a capable and committed helpmeet. If all that weren't bad enough, Jackson's huge "Tiger Spot" mosaic on the MU campus is crumbling as inexorably as his marriage.

Regular readers might remember that I once gently chastised Jackson for his so-called "Quartergate" crusade, in which he cast everyone from Gov. Bob Holden to the U.S. Mint as villains and liars and set himself up as a champion of artistic integrity.

It was a singularly whiny and pious piece of self-promotion, capped by a stunt whereby Jackson distributed quarter-size stickers with his own design to be pasted on the back of coins. Sometimes, he included quarters with the stickers.

"I stood up for something I believe in," he told the Tribune. "If anything, I became this strange folk hero who gives away money." Yeah, I've known a lot of newly divorced guys who see themselves in that light.

I suspect that Jackson will make out OK. He might be a suffering artist at the moment, but he's definitely not a starving artist. His people-pleasin' works sell for thousands of dollars a whack and no doubt will continue to do so.

The "Tiger Spot" is typical in aesthetics, if not in scale. The 30-foot-wide mosaic on Lowry Mall, right in front of MU Ellis Library, depicts the face of a tiger in thousands of pieces of Italian glass. It is potentially a very impressive work.

It has been plagued, however, by Missouri weather and other mysterious vagaries. Jackson said hammer-wielding vandals hit "Tiger Spot" shortly after its initial completion in autumn 2001. Water leaked in, and the mosaic has been a big eyesore pretty much ever since.

A lot of people insisted the mosaic would never work at that site, that the regular cycle of freezing, thawing, raining and roasting made it wholly impractical. Jackson has ignored the doubters, saying that the vandalism was what made the piece vulnerable to water damage.

I've always thought there was something fishy about the claims of vandalism. Who on Earth would do such a thing, and why would they select "Tiger Spot" as a target?

Jackson had some strong suspicions, which he reported to MU police. At least one blameless person I know—whose only crime was that he didn't get along with Jackson—was named by the artist as a suspect and had to undergo a police interrogation to clear his name. While Jackson was understandably upset, it was despicable of him to name suspects without a shred of supporting evidence.

Not just the mosaic but also the entire mall has been messed up for nearly two years. The mosaic is blocked off by yellow caution tape and shaded by a fading striped awning, producing an effect somewhere between a crime scene and a carny sideshow.

Jackson said he has been working feverishly to repair the mosaic and hopes to be finished by July 4. That would be a relief. The mosaic repair was threatening to turn into the longest-lasting art restoration project since Clive renovated the Taj Mahal.

I've walked by the site probably a half-dozen times a week for the past year, and I have seen Jackson actually working on it exactly once. If I had brought along a television camera crew, I might have had better luck.

On several occasions, however, I have seen university workers toiling on the project. Just last week, I saw Campus Design and Construction laborers laying commemorative bricks along the perimeter of the mosaic. I mention the point only because "Tiger Spot" has been repeatedly touted as a privately funded project. Taxpayers have already paid for special drainage work at the site, and I'd lay odds that those bricklayers I saw weren't unpaid volunteers.

As long as I'm in a betting mood, I'll wager that we'll be seeing renovations on the "Tiger Spot" for a long, long time to come. Informed sources tell me that it's likely the mosaic will eventually have to be protected by some sort of permanent roof, which would negate the work's effect by making it essentially the floor of a picnic shelter. It would also ruin the spacious, open quality of Lowry Mall.

There is an alternative to this grim scenario—a suggestion that could be filed under "Modest Proposals." Jackson could make a 30-foot-wide sticker emblazoned with a tiger head. Made of adhesive-backed, hammer-proof, water-resistant, non-fading vinyl, it would shelter and protect the "Tiger Spot" from sun, rain and vandals. All right, it probably isn't such a great idea, but it's no worse than the original notion of an open-air mosaic floor in the middle of Missouri.

They said it couldn't be done, and it looks like they might have been right.

Columbia: Where the slogan goes on and on

NOT TO BRAG, BUT MY EXPERIENCE IN THE FIELD OF GRAPHIC DESIGN GOES BACK decades, to a brilliantly productive term as assistant design editor of the Iowa City High School "Little Hawk," where I specialized in shadow-boxes and the overuse of spot color.

That expertise might not qualify me to criticize the professionals who designed the new logo for the Columbia Convention and Visitors Bureau, but two other things do: a column and a deadline.

Well, there is one other thing: namely a memory of the two basic principles of logo design: boldness and pith. The new logo has neither.

The logo design, reported to have cost $45,000 in public money, features the city's name in curlicue letters and the following tagline: "The smart, innovative, artsy, eclectic, clever, savvy, vibrant, too-dynamic-to-fit-into-a-short-tagline city."

The logo was conceived to appeal to young travelers, a bureau official said. Hmmm. Maybe I'm just in the wrong demographic.

In the interests of fairness, I took an "instant poll" of three teenagers who just happened to be in the house at the time, showing them the logo and asking, in uninflected tones, what they thought of it. The results were mixed: one vote for "cheesy," one for "fruit" and a third—from a lad who had trouble deciphering the tagline—for "stupid."

Granted, junior high boys are as tough a crowd as you can find anywhere. They reserve their enthusiastic approval almost exclusively for selected movies, sports teams and video games. Still, I believe their observations had merit.

The name of our fair city is rendered in a type font with an undeniable "flower power" feel, emphasized by the fact that the multicolored letters are laid out in a wavy line—a look originally inspired by the wide use of psychedelic drugs in the 1960s. It's kooky! It's trippy! It's really annoying!

Why in the name of all that is sensible does the chamber of commerce insist on pitching Columbia as the Berkeley of the Heartland? I've been to Berkeley, Calif., and Columbia is no Berkeley. Even if it were, would that be much of a selling point? Not to most people, and certainly not to me.

I like what we are: a small southern city whose moderate conservatism is tempered by the presence of a land-grant university. Hey, maybe that last phrase could be a tagline! It's only a little longer than the one they're using and a lot more informative.

The tagline is so cumbersome that it is unlikely to be read even in meter-high letters on a billboard. People whizzing by at 80 mph aren't going to pay attention to that much text. Let's hope the driver two car lengths ahead doesn't suddenly slow down so he can make sure to catch every artsy, eclectic, clever, vibrant, savvy word.

How did the firm of Woodruff Communications come up with this beast, anyway? "The tagline just grew into this unwieldy thing, and we thought it was kind of funny and memorable," a Woodruff senior writer said.

That's what happens when people with too few ideas sit around drinking too much coffee. My take is that the writer was so overwhelmed by Columbia's many virtues and attractions that he had trouble paring the list down to something reasonably snappy. Or maybe he's a not-clever-or-savvy-enough-to-come-up-with-a-tagline writer.

City slogans of this sort are intended to convey one message: "Stop here and spend money!"

Some towns base their slogans on an outstanding local feature: "The City Built on Cheese!" or "Widget Capital of the West!" or "Birthplace of 'Kato' Kaelin!"

Usually, however, literal meaning is less important than catchiness. A typical example would be, "Where the Past Meets the Future," which, when you think about it, applies to any point in the time-space continuum. My personal favorite slogan is that of Batavia, Iowa, whose hand-lettered billboard proclaims it "On the Way to Everywhere!"

Columbia could do worse than simply to list reasons to stop: "Parks, restaurants, shopping, museums, motels and more!" But who would pay $45,000 for something like that?

Besides, an epigrammatic quality is considered essential for billboard slogans. One that describes Columbia has to be comprehensive as well as terse. Just off-the-cuff, I'd suggest something along the lines of: "Columbia: Everything You Need—Anything You Want!" Or perhaps the ungrammatical but memorable: "Columbia: You Want It? We Got It!"

OK, those aren't the best. But neither do they come with a five-figure price tag.

One thing Columbia does have is a lot of bright, imaginative, thoughtful, quick-witted people—and by an amazing coincidence, every one of them reads this column! So, dear readers, brew up a latte, sharpen your ballpoints and send your slogan ideas to: Columbia Chamber of Commerce, 300 S. Providence Road, Columbia, Mo., 65203.

Columbia: We Can Do Better Than This.

Air-show arrest flips finger at 'freedom'

EVERY ONCE IN A WHILE, I LIKE TO PUT MY FEET ON THE HOB, LIGHT UP THE COB and muse on the meaning of freedom.

It's a word that has been kicked around lately to the point of serious debasement. Terrorists, we are told, hate our freedoms. Convenience stores promise freedom of choice, while car manufacturers offer freedom as part of the standard package.

Numerous correspondents scold me and others who are against the war in Iraq, reminding us that U.S. soldiers have died for our freedoms and for that reason we should not criticize the current government's policy.

It is a topsy-turvy perspective, demanding that freedom be foresworn out of respect for those who fought for it. Somewhere, George Orwell is smiling sardonically.

Nowhere has the paradox been more beautifully illustrated than at the Salute to Veterans Air Show at Columbia Regional Airport on Memorial Day weekend. It was, as the name implies, an event that paid tribute to those who paid the ultimate sacrifice for our freedoms—from the revolutionary Minutemen to the troops who even now are sweating out their extended tours of duty in the Middle East.

A sane and reasonable person might think the occasion the perfect time and place to exercise some of those hard-won freedoms, as long as the exercisers didn't disrupt the air show. After all, the airport is a publicly owned facility and the air show was open to all members of the public.

Unfortunately, sanity and reason—not to mention freedom—played distinctly subsidiary roles in the Salute to Veterans Air Show. Before it even took place, the city attorney said that the event would not be "a public forum of any kind. To the extent this property is a forum over Memorial Day weekend, it is a temporary private forum controlled by a private organization, the Salute to Veterans Corp.," he wrote. "The public has no right to exercise free speech activities in this area."

The emphasis on privacy is puzzling. The corporation was granted free use of the public airport. The event was promoted heavily on the city's public Web site, on the utility bills it sent out and even on its cable channel. Columbia police, Boone County Sheriff's deputies, Missouri State Highway Patrol troopers and airport personnel—not privately hired guards—provided security for the wing-ding.

And what security it was! When a Columbia man was observed passing a petition around at the event, police converged on him like he was taking a piddle in the middle of the tarmac. He was arrested, issued a summons for first-degree trespass and removed from the area. His petition, by the way, wasn't even about the war but about some issue involving city utilities.

Police also apprehended another desperado at the air show—a nun who was distributing small leaflets urging peace. She was not arrested but was "escorted" from the airport.

Whew, I feel freer already, knowing that our public servants are protecting us by arresting peaceful petitioners and frog-marching nuns off the premises. What really brings on the warm 'n' fuzzy emotions, though, is the knowledge that your tax dollars and mine are supporting the sort of heavy-handed tactics that would have brought a smile to the face of the flintiest commissar.

I noticed on my latest city utility bill—long after the event had come and gone—the notice that "no direct funds" went from city coffers to support the air show. This caveat appears to be in line with the contract between the city and the corporation, which states: "In no event shall the City and the Corporation be deemed or construed to be joint venturers or partners."

Yet, when one considers the in-kind contributions from the city, it's pretty hard to deem or construe them as anything else. What would it have cost the corporation to hire a security force equivalent to the publicly paid gendarmes on hand at the event? What would it have cost to do direct mailings to every utility customer in Columbia? What would it have cost to rent a facility like the airport?

At ciphering, I'm not so good, but I'd guess the total would be … a lot—far more, anyway, than the average annual salary of the typical tax-paying Tribune reader.

When it comes to the Salute to Veterans Air Show, "freedom" apparently means not having to pay for something. It certainly bears no resemblance to anything found in the Bill of Rights. I could have told you that for nothing.

What's Wal-Mart done for us lately?

MORE THAN A YEAR HAS PASSED SINCE I TOOK THE PUBLIC PLEDGE NEVER AGAIN to darken the door of a Wal-Mart store.

Admittedly, I have been tempted a time or two. Where else can you pick up a dozen eggs, a tack hammer, a car battery and an azalea bush all in one stop? Like a reformed alcoholic passing a liquor store, I've almost had to wrestle with the wheel to keep the car from steering itself into the parking lot.

It's a matter of convictions versus convenience, but so far I've been able to resist the pull and drive a little farther, even pay a little more, to support independently owned businesses that are being steamrolled by the Wal-Monster.

It's hard, however, to keep Wal-Mart completely out of one's consciousness. It keeps appearing in the news. For example, the recent publication of the list of richest Americans included a slew of Wal-Mart heirs, including the two heirs-in-law that call Columbia home: Stan Kroenke and Bill Laurie. No doubt their inclusion significantly boosts the average annual household income in our fair city.

But wait, there's more! What else has Wal-Mart done for us lately?

Well, it has poured oil in troubled waters—specifically thousands of gallons of nasty grease into Hinkson Creek from its grease traps behind the Supercenter on Conley Road.

Two 1,000-gallon grease traps installed in 1998 had never been pumped out, although that's supposed to happen every six months. The cost to Columbia taxpayers: $4,000 for cleanup, plus possible fines from the state that could be in five figures.

In response to a series of probing questions from Tribune reporter Dave Moore about the grease spill, the company blew him off thusly: "As this is a project that we are currently researching, coordinating and implementing, we would not be able to share any specifics of that project."

Maybe the Beast of Bentonville, Ark., has a long-range, nefarious plan to befoul the poor, "protected" Hinkson Creek beyond all hope of recovery. At the site of a planned new Supercenter on Columbia's southeast side, the developers wanted to fill a ravine with 2,500 dump-truck loads of dirt and build a parking lot on it.

A spoilsport from the state Department of Natural Resources pointed out that the plan would not be good for Hinkson Creek, so the developers came up with an alternative that would involve high retention walls and considerably less pollution. There is no problem, apparently, that can't be overcome by pouring more concrete.

Another Supercenter is planned for Columbia's west side. The 17 acres zoned for commercial use might not be enough. Wal-Mart hopes to add another 13 acres to the development, even though just about everyone who lives near the site is passionately opposed to the idea of a quarter-million-square-foot retail

Death Star that's open 24 hours a day, seven days a week. It will screw up traffic, light up the night sky and seriously depress home values. Not a single one of those complaining homeowners is a billionaire, however, so to hell with 'em.

The imminent closing of Osco Drug isn't technically Wal-Mart-related news, but Kroenke bought the property in April, and the store definitely constitutes competition with the monster. I have, in fact; patronized it often during my personal Wal-Mart boycott. A spokesperson for the store told the Tribune she believes Kroenke's lease renewal terms were intended to drive the 35-year-old emporium out of business.

It's one thing to keep building unnecessary, stream-polluting, minimum-wage-paying, union-busting Supercenters. It's quite another to buy up property and deliberately put a downtown institution such as Osco's out of business. How does that contribute to the health and well-being of our community?

If I keep going on like this, I'm bound to be accused of nattering negativity. On the bright side, a lot of Wal-Mart lucre went into the building of the new University of Missouri-Columbia basketball facility, Paige Sports Arena. For the big inaugural event, they're bringing in—are you ready for this?—The Village People and Cher!

There's some real cultural enrichment for you. Me, I'd rather just go to Osco's.

Wal-Mart rant was nothing personal

THINK YOUR VOTE DOESN'T MEAN ANYTHING? TRY WRITING A WEEKLY NEWSPAPER column! You spend agonizing hours wringing your soul all over the page, working out thoughtful themes and irrefutable arguments—and nothing happens.

Usually, that is, nothing happens, aside from the occasional mildly corrective or approving message. Rarely do I experience a public paddling like I did on Sunday's editorial page, where Tribune publisher and grand vizier Hank Waters took me out behind the woodshed.

Hank wrote that my recent rant about Wal-Mart was "gratuitous and unfair."

I ought to be smarting, I suppose, but I have to confess that as spankings go this one was tolerable. My first reaction to the headline—"Be fair to Wal-Mart"—was to leap up and exclaim, "It bleeds! The Wal-monster bleeds!"

No doubt I flatter myself with the conceit that members of the local Wal-Mart plutocracy—some of the richest people in the world—were personally annoyed, however momentarily, by my spirited comments. It was probably just their lawyer. Nevertheless, I cherish this illusion. I never could seem to get a rise out of Richard Mellon Scaife.

That said, I was probably wrong to take at face value the published words of an Osco Drug employee implying that Wal-Mart was deliberately trying to drive the store out of business. Maybe Osco spurned a perfectly reasonable offer from Wal-Mart scion Stan Kroenke that would have allowed the venerable downtown mercantile to stay open and operational.

Still, what I see on the face of it is another smaller central-city store closing down while Wal-Mart Supercenters open up right next to residential neighborhoods. Even if there's no direct cause and effect, the larger trend is undeniable, and it's easy to get upset about the way it affects people's lives.

For instance, I was probably just upset when I wrote in my offending column that Wal-Mart seems to have a long-range plan to pollute Hinkson Creek. Or maybe I was just being facetious.

In any case, the point I was trying to make is that any enormous international corporation—not just Wal-Mart—has a primary fiduciary responsibility to its shareholders. If the company finds that the cost of polluting—including fines, cleanup and bad publicity—is less than the cost of not polluting, the company will pollute. This general proposition has, sadly, been exhaustively documented.

To be sure, Wal-Mart has fairly close community ties to Columbia because several of the firm's major players actually live here, although not within car-horn range of a Supercenter. They seem to be solid, contributing citizens, and I have nothing against them personally. Surely they have no say in the facility's handling of sewage and probably no awareness of what's going on at the Wal-Mart stores in Buber, Mont., or Schopenhauer, Texas, or wherever their retail juggernaut happens to be rolling along.

No, my quarrel isn't with the Kroenkes or the Lauries. It's Wal-Mart I can't stand.

It does bother me on a purely emotional level that the local gazillionaires ultimately seem to get the authorities to go along with whatever they want in terms of development. But that, I suppose, is like pointlessly objecting to the fact that money can overcome almost any obstacle.

On the other hand, as Hank puts it, "Wal-Mart arguably has a harder row to hoe because of the strain of anti-company sentiment it faces." That's encouraging. It might be futile to rage against the tide, but it's still possible to swim against it just by taking your trade to stores outside the big boxes.

As members of the greater Columbia community, we all should try to shop at locally owned and operated stores, to buy local food when possible and purchase goods made right here in Central Missouri.

Granted, such an idealized shopping regimen can get pretty complicated and expensive if carried to extremes. Maybe we should start with something easy. How about we begin by buying all our Halloween stuff somewhere other than Wal-Mart?

If that proves doable, the next logical step is to make out a Wal-Mart-free Christmas shopping list. After that, I have an excellent suggestion for a New Year's resolution. ...

If my enmity toward Wal-Mart seems a little crazed, well, what can I say? It drives me crazy! And I know I'm not alone. "Be fair to Wal-Mart!" might work fine as a headline, but it doesn't have much future as a popular slogan.

Embarrassment is a fair price to pay

ATTENTION, WAL-MART SHOPPERS! THOSE BLUE LIGHTS ARE FLASHING AGAIN, which means another big embarrassment in our public image department!

As if there weren't already enough reasons to shop anywhere else, it now appears that hard-earned money you spent at Wal-Mart has been going to subsidize academic cheating on the part of local heiress Paige Laurie.

It was only a few weeks ago that the daughter of Bill and Nancy Laurie graced the ribbon-cutting ceremony of the University of Missouri-Columbia sports facility for which her parents partially paid and that bears her name.

At the Paige Sports Arena opening, she seemed a charming and comely lass, although the peroxide was a shade too vivid for my taste. Me-ow! Actually, her startling blondness is probably attributable to time spent in the sun, for she has been attending the University of Southern California.

When she was only a freshman there, according to the ABC program "20/20," she began paying her roommate to write her papers and complete her homework assignments. The roommate, Elena Martinez, told "20/20" she even performed such tasks as going to a play Laurie was required to attend, then turning over the ticket stubs to Laurie so she could prove to her professor that she'd been to the production.

Martinez said the arrangement continued for 3 ½ years, with a cumulative payoff of about $20,000. She provided ABC with extensive documentation to back up her sordid story, including e-mails, assignments and even a videotape.

In a twist that could be called ironic, Columbians didn't get to view the "20/20" segment because it was pre-empted by the local affiliate in favor of the MU men's basketball game at Paige Sports Arena—a humiliating loss, as it turned out, to unheralded Davidson. Maybe the coincidence was less ironic than it was karmic. The men's basketball program was itself recently penalized for cheating, its recruiting practices being deemed in violation of NCAA rules.

In response to the program, the Laurie family issued a terse comment: "Paige Laurie's college record is a private matter." The statement was completely appropriate, although a sad example of locking the barn door way too late. That horse hasn't just escaped: It's enjoying a fruity rum drink on a sunny beach in a country that has no extradition treaty.

The fact is that Laurie's college record is now literally national news. It might be strictly private in the most technical sense, but jeez, try telling that to Monica Lewinsky.

A lot of people might contend that all the news coverage—even this insignificant little commentary—is terribly unfair to Laurie, a 22-year-old undergraduate who did only what thousands of college students do as a matter of routine. After all, the "20/20" story in its entirety was about the prevalence of college cheating, usually in the form of Internet plagiarizing.

What is unusual and even newsworthy, however, is paying someone $20,000 to write your papers, do your homework and attend your plays.

So let's talk about fairness. Is it unfair to devote so much television and ink to a relatively minor miscreant just because she happens to be rich and sort of semifamous? Maybe. Is it unfair for that rich and famous person to pay someone to cheat for her? Definitely!

A degree from a prestigious university such as USC is said to translate into millions of dollars in anticipated income over a lifetime. To attain that degree by devious means is akin to stealing considerable sums from future employers who think they're hiring someone with an honest-to-God college education. Is that fair?

From the sound of it, Elena Martinez is someone who could really have used that extra income a USC degree could generate. As a confessed cheater, she'll never get one now, even though she appears to have the requisite brains and ability. Despite her ill-gotten gains, she had to leave the school because she couldn't afford the tuition, she said. She now attends a community college. So much for the meritocracy, eh?

Paige Laurie doesn't really need any more money than the billions she stands to inherit. It would be interesting to know whether USC intends to let her keep her spuriously gained baccalaureate, or whatever it is. Either way, she's never going to run short of cash, and if her self-esteem demands that she embark on a career of some sort, with her connections she's pretty well assured of that, too.

In short, the only meaningful penalty that can be meted out for her alleged transgressions is the scalding embarrassment she is enduring right now. In spite of her looks, her money and all her other advantages, I don't really envy her at the moment. But it seems only fair.

Trolley-bus idea reeks of faux-thenticity

THIS ALWAYS HAPPENS DURING THE HOLIDAY SEASON. WHEN THE DAYS TURN gloomy, the nights get longer in duration and old wounds start to throb like jungle drums, I get a little bit cranky. That's all it is.

Nah, I'm just romancing. My grumpiness at the moment stems from my belief that spending $60,000 for two "trolley-style" city buses is an idea that crosses the line of "clever" and strays far into the territory of "cute."

The Columbia city government is prepared to buy two para-transit vans designed to serve disabled passengers, two new city buses and a couple of bus shelters, with 80 percent of the money coming from federal funds and the rest from city coffers.

Some municipal officials, Mayor Darwin Hindman foremost among them, would like to buy a couple of buses decked out to look like trolley cars and designated to serve the downtown Columbia area, also known as—Bah, humbug!—The District.

A few of our beloved mayor's ideas tend to bring the latent Scrooge in me bubbling to the surface. For the record, I have never voted against him, and I'm generally happy to join in the hosannas evoked by the mention of his name. But every once in a while, he uncomfortably reminds me of those old teen movies starring Mickey Rooney: "Hey, gang, I've got a great idea: Let's buy some buses and trick 'em out like old trolleys! My mom will make the costumes! We'll sell tickets! Hooray!"

If the faux-trolley idea at first seems strictly goofy, it's worth remembering that every visionary idea is initially regarded as idiotic, subversive or both. The notion of buses disguised as old-time trolleys has real appeal, but only if it would involve open-air, step-on-the-running-board-and-hang-on riding, such as the cars from central San Francisco to North Beach. No way, though. The liability alone makes it impractical.

So, these would be counterfeit trolleys, monuments to the cosmetic aesthetic. What would be the point of them? Why, a high-profile advertisement for the Good Life in Columbia: The Too-Broke-to-Build-a-Sidewalk-in-My-Neighborhood-but-Can-Afford-a-Phony-Funny-Trolley-Kinda-Cuddly-Little-City! Did I get that slogan wrong again?

Trolley-buses would be useful maybe a dozen times a year, to shuttle wealthy alumni to and from Harpo's and the Norm E. "Paige" Stewart Memorial Mizzou Pavilion. And you would definitely want to fire them up when the editors of Money magazine came to town. Maybe, eventually, I could grow to like them.

I doubt it. They would only remind that times are kind of tight at the moment. More state and federal programs are getting cut, which will further increase the burdens borne by local government. That, in turn, means higher local taxes.

Only last week, there was public discussion about a possible new excise tax for new development on the city fringes, plus increases in sales, real estate and personal property taxes. And those were just for city road repair and construction. There were other urgent needs as well: ice-melting electrical elements for the public library steps; affordable housing in central Columbia; pollution protection for Rock Bridge Memorial State Park; financial assistance for families who can't afford to use city recreational facilities; a tax on online sales; a new county-city health clinic, a city health museum …

I neither damn nor endorse these proposals and projects here, only offer them as a partial list of real or potential drains on local public resources—in addition to the ongoing payrolls and potholes.

It's true that the federal/city tax money to pay for trolley-buses is separate and unrelated to, say, the state-administered federal grant that will enable Rock Bridge Park to pump its wastewater to the Columbia treatment plant. All of it, however, ultimately derives from the same source: the public pocketbook. And the jolly-trolley idea just strikes me as sort of extravagant.

Still, few Columbians would want that federal transit money for the city to go unclaimed. Well, hold on to your beanies, gang, because I have a great idea!

Actually, it's not my idea: It's something Columbia did for a short time years ago, then abandoned. The city converted several buses to run on a biodiesel fuel mixture instead of straight diesel. The mixture was said to have remarkable properties of lubricity, lengthening engine life significantly.

More important, perhaps, the biodiesel buses didn't give off that foul, industrial diesel stink. Instead, they smelled like popping popcorn. Not only was it a big improvement in the olfactory department; it was environmentally responsible and good for farmers.

I'll bet more people would ride the city buses if they didn't reek like the farts of Thor. And you know, the only really ugly bus is a big, old empty bus.

So, what are we waiting for? Put in that paperwork with the feds and cut a deal with MFA! Get the Missouri Soybean Merchandising Council on board, and somebody call the Farm Bureau! We'll soon have every bus stop in this town smelling like a theater lobby.

It's visionary, I tell you! My mom'll make the costumes.

The columnist personifies war's ferocious face at a mid-Missouri military "museum" in the late 1980s.

CHAPTER 6

AMERICA GOES TO WAR

Terrorist crimes call for justice, not war

"We're at war," President George W. Bush announced last weekend. In the same speech, he said, "We will find those who did it, we will smoke them out of their holes, we will get them running and we will bring them to justice."

Please, Mr. President. We don't want war. We want justice. We want to see the guilty tried and punished.

The president has called up the reserves. He has cut a deal with Pakistan to let us use that country as a staging ground for airstrikes and ground invasions of Afghanistan, whose leaders are accused of aiding and abetting prime suspect Osama bin Laden in his campaigns of terror.

Does this mean war? Perhaps. Would war advance the cause of justice? Probably not.

To make war successfully would require a different set of circumstances, among them a new constitution. The document we're currently stuck with says only Congress can declare war, which hasn't happened for almost 60 years. If we do go to war, it would be refreshing to have it debated and voted upon in the constitutionally mandated manner.

Another thing war demands is a clearly defined enemy to attack. We aren't going to get bin Laden and his cohorts with airstrikes. We won't even be able to slay the Taliban leaders that way. You think those guys don't have bomb shelters? They have bomb shelters in their bomb shelters.

Consequently, airstrikes would kill a lot of innocent civilians but wouldn't touch the bad guys. Wouldn't that kind of put us on the level of ... Osama bin Laden? Furthermore, from every smoking crater, for every freshly martyred Afghani, two or two dozen more new recruits would arise—ready to devote their lives to the jihad against the United States.

Ground troops, then! Could we not invade in force and take them with our powerful infantry and artillery? Maybe. On the other hand, Afghanistan is not Grenada. It's not even Panama or Iraq. We in the United States like to believe we were responsible for the breakup of the Soviet Union. But Afghanistan was the anvil that broke the hammer and sickle.

It's possible that Bush's presidential declaration of war is a gigantic bluff. If so, I pray that it succeeds. I take the point that any threat of war, to be credible, must be accompanied by a conscientiously applied program of vigorous saber-rattling and bloodcurdling rhetoric.

In the meantime, the federal law enforcement machinery appears to be doing a professional job of evidence-gathering. The Taliban has promised cooperation if the United States can produce convincing evidence that the guilty parties are within Afghanistan's borders.

Let us find that evidence and produce it. Combined with military, financial and political pressure, it might be enough to persuade the Afghans to expel bin Laden from their country, if not actually to hand him over at the frontier.

Let's also call upon the International Criminal Tribunal to aid us in our search. It got Slobodan Milosevic; perhaps it can be of service in the hunt for bin Laden and his gang. It's curious that none of our leaders has so much as mentioned it.

The awful events of last week have, at least temporarily, won us the sympathy and support of almost all nations. We have an opportunity to build a coalition based on respect for the rule of law. While making clear our bedrock support of Israeli nationhood, we need to embrace the involvement of the Islamic countries in this quest for justice.

Most of them have already denounced the terrorist attacks, at least in their official statements. Even fundamentalist theocracies revere the principle of the rule of law, just so long as they're the ones making the laws. They don't like troublemakers, and this bin Laden individual is big trouble.

If bin Laden were on the lam, would any country offer him a safe haven? The odds are not great, considering the potentially devastating consequences.

They don't want war, either.

Do we really want war? It's been said that politicians and generals are always planning for the previous war. While it seems almost unpatriotic to mention it now, two weeks ago the men who lead us were planning for a war in which North Korea would launch a nuclear missile at Seattle. The $300 billion missile shield they envisioned won't protect us from zealots with box-cutters.

"We are going to get them," Bush vowed, "no matter what it takes."

It will take more than missiles and cannons, more than airstrikes and infantry and artillery. It will take patience, stealth and cunning.

I hope we have those weapons in our arsenal.

Let's not fall for Bush's bait-and-switch

ALMOST EVERYONE HAS ENCOUNTERED OR AT LEAST HEARD OF THE ILLEGAL practice, once a common retailing strategy, in which a store advertises an item for sale at a very low price, but the customers who respond are buttonholed by a salesperson who tells them the last advertised item has just been sold, "but we do have some other extremely attractive values. ..."

This hoary old ploy is known as the bait-and-switch. I don't know whether a specific term exists to describe the equivalent of bait-and-switch in foreign policy. There should be such a term, the better to describe what President George W. Bush and his advisers are trying to put over on the American public.

When the country was in a state of emotional hemorrhage from the events of Sept. 11, Bush laid the blame squarely on the narrow shoulders of one Osama bin Laden, evil mastermind of the al-Qaida network. We will find him, Bush promised, and we will punish him for his horrific crimes. "Dead or alive," the president pledged, and Dick Cheney said the same, along with Donald Rumsfeld and all the rest.

Six months later, bin Laden remains at large. Only the rhetoric has changed. Perhaps you saw the Associated Press story in Thursday's Tribune under the headline: "Bin Laden irrelevant, Bush says." Asked about bin Laden at a news conference, Bush said, "I am truly not that concerned about him." The account did not say whether the president stifled a yawn, but it did quote him as saying: "I am deeply concerned about Iraq."

Aha! The old bait-and-switch: Bin Laden was the bait, Saddam Hussein the switch.

The body count from Sept. 11 will be forever uncertain, but the latest estimates put it, I believe, at something more than 3,000 people. It is the gravest single act of mass murder in history. Six months is an exceedingly brief statute of limitations for such a crime.

The Bush administration strained mightily to prove that bin Laden was behind the bombings. It finally seemed to have assembled a case that was convincing, if not ironclad. So why is it that bringing him to justice is no longer a high priority? What about the president's promise? I read his lips very clearly. What happened to "dead or alive"?

Maybe bin Laden never really was the primary target. When the United States began bombing Afghanistan, the stated reason was to destroy his power base and "smoke him out of his hole." In these pages I mused at the time that other motives might be involved and that one of them could be "Poppy" Bush's unfinished business with Saddam.

Many readers responded with wounding calls and letters that questioned my analysis and even my patriotism. For the record, my antennae are up; you all can transmit your apologies telepathically. George II now freely admits that getting rid of Saddam is his primary concern.

Bush has tied his international policy securely to the removal of Saddam.

That is tantamount to a declaration of war, for if the Iraqi dictator is still in power as of November 2004, Bush will lose the presidency.

As politicians rhetorically expand the theater of operations, what's actually happening on the ground in Afghanistan, where the real war is being fought?

U.S. troops are still "mopping up" after a two-week battle dubbed Operation Anaconda, which was aimed at uprooting al-Qaida fighters in eastern Afghanistan. "Operation Anaconda is an incredible success," a U.S. military spokesman declared. "We've killed hundreds."

But a top allied Afghan commander in the region strongly disputed that rosy assessment. "Americans don't listen to anyone," he said. "Most people escaped—you can't call that a success. In my opinion, the campaign failed."

Whom to believe? Well, U.S. military authorities based their estimates on "an intelligence report that said that during the fight, al-Qaida commanders sent word to a nearby village to prepare hundreds of coffins."

According to the Afghan, "We don't put our dead in boxes." One has to wonder: Didn't it occur to U.S. intelligence agents to ask about local burial customs if they were going to make them the basis of an intelligence report? Apparently, it didn't.

Let's sum up: We are involved in an undeclared war in an Asian country a lot of Americans still can't locate on a map. Our commanders boast of tactical successes against an elusive guerilla enemy. Our native allies-in-arms, who comprehend the region far more thoroughly than our own intelligence services, do not share the sunny American outlook. In the meantime, Washington policy-makers seek to spread the conflict across borders, into other countries and other continents. The president calls for huge increases in defense spending. He says more troops will be needed, but victory is certain.

Does the preceding have an ominously familiar ring?

Out first duty as Americans is not to recite the Pledge of Allegiance or enlist in the army, to serve on a jury or even to pay our taxes. Our primary duty as citizens of this democratic republic is to pay attention. As free men and women, we are obligated to compare the words of our leaders with their actions, to question and criticize and to vote according to the dictates of our consciences.

We can't afford to fall for the bait-and-switch.

War on Iraq opens gate to mischief

"See, we love freedom, and that's what they don't understand. They hate things; we love things. They act out of hatred. We don't seek revenge; we seek justice out of love."

Would you be surprised to hear that the statement above was the utterance of a syntactically confused fourth-grader? No, you've probably already figured out that it's a verbatim quote from President George W. Bush, explaining to an Oklahoma City audience on Aug. 29 the reasons behind the war on terrorism and his proposal to expand it into Iraq.

Patriotic Americans should be glad the president had a couple of weeks to polish his message before he presented it to the United Nations last week. Though more prettily phrased, to be sure, it reflected the same dubious premises, the same stubborn illogic, the identical daffy conclusion: The United States must make war on Saddam Hussein's Iraq, with or without U.N. support or consent.

Why must we invade Iraq in defiance of the United Nations? Because Saddam has defied the United Nations!

The contradiction has not gone unnoticed by the rest of the world. Bush has chosen simply to ignore it. Under the headline "Bush mocks naysayers," the Associated Press reported how Bush ridiculed the notion of "waiting for the U.N. to act." He added with a chuckle: "I can't imagine an elected member of the U.S." Congress "saying, 'I think I'm going to wait for the United Nations to make a decision.'"

Bush's open scorn for the United Nations shouldn't come as a big surprise. No administration in our history has been so cynically unconcerned about international conventions and treaties. From the Kyoto Protocol to the International Conference on Racism, SALT II and the world court: Every attempt at practical cooperation is sacrificed in the interests of the short-term grab.

It's a risky strategy for the new global millennium, but Bush and his boys seem to believe that the United States, as the sole surviving superpower, can do pretty much whatever it pleases. If only that were true!

Certainly, no other two or even three powers combined can match the military might and economic clout of Uncle Sam. As we can see from the current situation, however, it doesn't require another superpower to create an international crisis. Heck, even Iraq can do it!

Saddam used to be the big bully in the regional bloc, mostly because the United States pumped him up for his war on Iran. Since a U.S.-led coalition thrashed and thumped his Republican Army in the Gulf War, he was been considerably weaker. His military machine is hamstrung, his nation's economy crippled by sanctions. There are large parts of his own country he can't fly over. Even Vice President Dick Cheney now admits that Iraq has neither nuclear weapons nor the means to deliver them.

And yet, Iraqi "regime change" is deemed absolutely crucial to vital U.S. interests. It's not that Saddam isn't a brutal dictator; he's just not all that powerful outside central Iraq.

If a weakened Iraq can cause all this mischief, think of what other countries with far greater resources might be able to do. It has already moved beyond the hypothetical. The Russians have announced that they will bomb and invade parts of the independent Republic of Georgia, which they accuse of harboring Chechnyan rebels—or terrorists, as the Russians refer to them.

Assume the United States and its submissive handmaiden, Great Britain, launch a war without international approval or even acquiescence. The gate would be open for any nation to pursue its own agenda aggressively. Think of India settling the Kashmir question or of China finally putting the Tibetans in their place and maybe even muscling up in the Formosan straits.

Conventional constraints and the rule of law would no longer apply, but that's not the only thing. The United States could protest against the action of these other countries, and that's about all. Our military would be otherwise engaged in and around greater metropolitan Baghdad.

What hope remains for peace? Plenty, actually. Saddam has already largely capitulated in the matter of weapons inspections. The major remaining sticking point is whether the U.N. inspection team shall be accompanied by a detachment of armed U.S. forces. Other countries' soldiers, OK, but not the Americans.

This seems to me to be a negotiable point, not necessarily worth a $50 billion war. That's a conservative estimate, by the way. No war in history has ever come in under budget. What makes a peaceful settlement less likely is the declared U.S. intent to oust Saddam from power. To that, he will never agree.

Finally, let it be noted that the combined efforts of all U.S. and allied intelligence services have been unable to produce a single shred of evidence tying the Iraqi regime to the terrorist attacks of Sept. 11, 2001.

Oh. Right. That. The evildoer who allegedly masterminded them has not yet been brought to book, despite the presidential assurances of a year ago. The wanted posters for Laden, O. b., now read: "Dead or Alive?"

I could be wrong, but I think that means he got away.

'Peace and goodwill' more than a slogan

EVERY PATRIOTIC AMERICAN KNOWS THE MIDDLE EAST IS A TROUBLOUS AND tumultuous place, home to enormous reserves of fossil fuel, the birthplace of Jesus and two-thirds of the "axis of evil." Keeping all those factors in mind, we blithely observe the birthday of the Prince of Peace even as we prepare to rain fire and steel upon faraway Iraq.

Most of us have only a vague conception of the Middle East—a vast area stretching from Algeria east to the western borders of India, populated by rival religionists bent on blowing one another up. Some of them want to blow us up, too.

Despite the fact that the Middle East is in our headlines every day, we remain hazy on its geography—full of tiny, confusing sovereignties such as Qatar and Yemen. The typical American can't even locate Belgium on a map. Try Bahrain.

Maybe by this time, a lot of people can pinpoint Iraq. As we hear nightly on the newscasts, of all the horrible and repressive regimes in the world, Iraq is deemed the first among evils. To us, it seems like a barren, forsaken place—a stony landscape baked by the merciless Saharan sun and ruled by a brutal despot.

It is also the cradle of civilization, this place we are about to bomb back into the Stone Age. I'm only marginally better in history than I am in geography, but I remember that the Fertile Crescent between the Tigris and Euphrates rivers was where agriculture began. That Sumerian development was more important to the evolution of modern civilization than the discovery of the wheel and almost as important as the taming of fire.

Cultivation of the land meant men and women didn't have to spend all their time hunting and gathering and could instead devote some of their energies to other activities. Among the secondary Sumerian innovations were writing, weaving and brewing.

We Americans take just pride in our technological know-how. We gave the world the automobile, the airplane, the light bulb and the television, to name only a few. But that doesn't begin to stack up with the contributions of the folks in the Euphrates Valley.

Is it possible that the Middle Easterner's lack of affection for Americans might stem in part from our easy assumptions of superiority? We Yankees generally mean well, but we tend to be pushy in advocating ways we could improve things. We meddle. People who have been doing those things a certain way for about 6,000 years might reasonably resent the implication that we white Westerners know better. They are likely to resist change.

Besides all those useful things that sprang from ancient Sumerian civilization, the Middle East is also the anvil upon which half the world's major religions were forged. In the relatively small territory popularly known as the Holy Land, precious sacred sites are as common as Casey's stores are over here.

Among the holiest of them is, of course, Bethlehem, site of the Nativity we celebrate tonight.

At any rate, continuing disputes concerning title and access to these places is the basis for much of the bloodshed we see today. While many of them lack the name recognition or spiritual significance to Westerners of Bethlehem, they apparently have great strategic value. U.S. military forces occupy some of them, a matter much resented by many Muslims, including Osama bin Laden and his followers.

Jesus urged us all to walk in the shoes of another—to understand pain and the passions that we don't necessarily share. Maybe, on this holiday at least, we ought to try. Otherwise, we might as well admit that peace and goodwill are concepts we like to confine to our Christmas cards.

Should U.S. cut the French connection?

Boy, THOSE FRENCH REALLY BURN ME UP, WITH THEIR LITTLE MUSTACHES AND whimsical hats and their fancy French cooking.

Well, from now on you can hold the foie gras and super-size my Freedom fries because we, the American people, are hopping mad at France's refusal to link arms with us and march to Baghdad. France has even threatened to use its veto power in the U.N. Security Council to stop a war resolution. Sacre blooey!

This snooty attitude, so typically Gallic, brings my Scotch-Irish-Dutch-German blood to a patriotic boil. Why can't the French just cooperate, for once? Don't they know what they owe us?

Twice in the past century, we have turned the tide against their German invaders. We also gave them Jerry Lewis, and although many Americans do not realize it, Pepe Le Pew is actually an American creation!

Thus confronted, the Frenchman would reply, in his snobby way, that his country did not trade Nazi occupation for the status of a vassal state in the American empire. "As for World War I, we Frenchmen held off the Huns for years and took millions of casualties. You Yanks arrive just in time to witness the German collapse and impregnate thousands of mademoiselles, you feelthy, uncultured poufs!"

That is what my Frenchman would say, although he'd probably pretend not to speak any English at all, just to make us feel stupid. They're so arrogant!

Just wait. We'll show them what arrogant is!

My newfound Franco-phobia generated a teeny bit of friction between me and the coquette who sometimes lets me use her hairbrush. She happens to be a big fan of all things French, including their stubborn insistence that a peaceful solution is the best possible course in Iraq.

"You know, the fact that France has been invaded twice in the past 90 years might be part of the reason they're not so gung-ho about invading someone else," she told me. "They know about the consequences in a way Americans don't. We've been attacked but never invaded."

Those are reasonable words, on the surface. But I think it's only fair to point out that her opinion is greatly colored by her pre-existing partiality for French cooking—a subject on which she has considerable expertise. This factor put me at an unfair disadvantage, as dinnertime was fast approaching. But when she pressed on, remarking on her preference for French wines, I came uncorked.

"You can take your swell Burgundies and Beaujolais and store 'em somewhere where the sun doesn't shine!" I bawled. "I'd put our fine Missouri screw-top vintages up against any one of 'em!"

And do you know what the creature did? She laughed—a horridly superior, odious, obviously French kind of laugh!

Ooooh ... We were first to da moon, Alice!

Not having a good comeback ready, I resolved to hit the history books and dredge up some useful facts about Franco-American relations, especially as they related to French ingratitude, cowardice and treachery.

It wasn't long before I found the flaw in her argument: Contrary to her statement, America has, too, been invaded!

The trouble with that nugget of information, however, was that the British were the invaders and the French were on our side. In fact, if the French Navy hadn't kept Lord Cornwallis bottled up at Yorktown, Va., Gen. Washington— and Lafayette—could not successfully have taken the town and won the American Revolutionary War.

About 20 years later, the French Emperor Napoleon, strapped for cash, unloaded the Louisiana Territory to the U.S. government for what amounted to a mess of pottage. For the bargain price of $15 million, they gave us about a quarter of the whole continent, including the land that contains the greater part of the Tribune readership.

During the American Civil War, the French contribution was defined by what the country didn't do. French refusal to recognize the Confederate States of America in any official diplomatic sense was a crucial factor in the Union's calculations and its eventual victory. Isn't that just like the French, though? To take credit for doing nothing!

All the same, I was starting to think that maybe the French weren't really our enemies after all. Sure, they're kind of stuck up, but they're not so bad when you get to know their history.

Then I read the words of President Dwight Eisenhower on April 7, 1954, when he coined the phrase "falling dominoes" to describe the imminent spread of communism in Southeast Asia if French colonialism were to collapse in Vietnam.

Exactly one month later, the French colonial stronghold of Dien Bien Phu fell. In July, the French withdrew, handed the conflict over to the United States and managed to stay well out of it for the next 20 years. What a dirty trick to play on an ally! But smart, you have to admit, in an Old Europe sort of way.

On balance, it seems like maybe we ought to try to keep France more or less on our side, even if we have to make some concessions. Why should we be surprised that the French favor more arms inspections and more and more talks? Talking is a French specialty; it's what makes them such successful diplomats and lovers.

I just wish they'd do it in plain, simple American English!

Bush fibs set bad example for children

THERE WAS A LOT OF CONCERN A FEW YEARS AGO ABOUT THE POTENTIAL EFFECTS on America's children of an untruthful president. I had hoped things were getting better until I asked my teenage son a simple question: "Have you done your math homework assignments?"

He gazed at me from under shaggy bangs: "I've been engaging in math-homework-assignment-program-related activities."

A thorough on-site inspection, however, revealed no evidence of actual completed homework.

So, I'm worried about the example President George W. Bush is setting for our children. Less than a year ago, he was declaring: "We know Iraq has weapons of mass destruction." Now he's using the milk-and-water characterization "weapons-of-mass-destruction-program-related-activities" while the actual weapons remain as elusive as the Holy Grail.

A lie is a lie, so does it matter what the liar lies about? No one assigns equivalent weight to every lie. For example, "Honey, those vinyl Capri pants make your butt look too small" might be a lie. It differs in motive and magnitude from statements like: "By far the vast majority of my tax cuts go to people at the bottom end of the economic ladder."

Bill Clinton lied straight out about an act of consensual sodomy. Many people, including President Bush, believe the United States faces a consensual sodomy crisis that could destroy the institution of marriage unless we pass a constitutional amendment—and quickly!

Other people, like me, think taking the nation to war is a more serious matter. Bush asserted repeatedly that we had to invade Iraq because Saddam Hussein had huge stockpiles of horrible weapons. We went to war. There were no weapons. Now, Bush uses weasel words to obliterate the distinction between truth and falsehood.

The fibs of the present administration are subtler, perhaps, but certainly no less insidious than those of the last. And Clinton ultimately did cop to his sordid fling with an Oval Office intern—staining, so to speak, an otherwise honorable legacy.

Bush, in contrast, just keeps piling up lies like cordwood. Only last week, he said: "We know Saddam was a growing danger."

Say what? Saddam was a tyrannical lunatic, all right, but all the evidence indicates he was a shrinking danger, not a growing one. Most of his vaunted military arsenal—sold to him largely by us—was used up or destroyed by the mid-1990s. By the time Bush II was installed in the White House, the Iraqi dictator's fearsome weapons existed almost entirely in his increasingly unhinged mind.

I meant Saddam's mind, not Bush's. Interestingly, though, a few members of the Bush administration—Dick Cheney foremost among them—are still operating under the assumption/illusion that the dreaded chemical and biological weapons are out there waiting to be found.

And if they aren't, the blame is said to rest entirely with the U.S. intelligence services, which consistently supplied the Bush White House with information that, for the most part, turned out to be spectacularly wrong. It wasn't only the weapons stuff, either, but also the notion that ordinary Iraqis would welcome the invading troops with open arms—not with small-arms fire.

By last weekend, even Bush was admitting that something was seriously flawed in the pre-pre-emptive war intelligence estimates, and he announced he was establishing an independent investigation to get to the bottom of it.

The investigation must be thorough, administration sources say, so it will probably take close to a year to complete the process. That means the truth—ha!—won't be revealed until well after the November elections. That's pretty convenient timing for candidate Bush.

Presumably, we already know which intelligence turned out to be wrong, which sources supplied it, and to whom. Why would an investigation take so long? There are several possible reasons.

Remember how Bush fought against a commission that would look into the events leading up to Sept. 11, 2001? And after he finally caved in, remember his choice to head up this truth-seeking body? It was Henry Kissinger—not exactly an exemplar of honesty and transparency in government. We don't know yet whom Bush will appoint to direct the investigation into prewar intelligence failures—Adm. John Poindexter, perhaps?

An Associated Press report published yesterday can't do much to reassure the public. The story quoted a senior White House official as saying the inquiry "would be patterned after the Warren Commission."

The Warren Commission investigated for 10 months and determined that Lee Harvey Oswald was the lone assassin of President John F. Kennedy. Forty years later, according to a Gallup poll, 80 percent of Americans still don't believe it.

That's setting a pretty low standard of credibility—the only standard this administration can realistically expect to meet.

Success hard to judge in murky mission

OUR LITTLE GREEN PLANET HAS CIRCLED THE SUN EXACTLY ONCE SINCE THE launching of "Shock and Awe," the first-ever openly pre-emptive war in the history of our glorious republic. The strict tenets of the Columnists Code require a retrospective article to mark the first anniversary of—just about anything.

One year later, we occupy Iraq, which in the traditionalist view would make us the winners, right? But as President George W. Bush has said, this is a new kind of war, and our current situation doesn't really feel very victorious. In fact, we literally can't wait to get out of Iraq and have vowed to leave by July 1, no matter what.

Iraq is a battleground marked by moving targets, shifting sands and even shiftier motivations. As we look back, we should ask: What were our goals? Did we reach them? And finally, what difference did it make?

One goal that has been at least partly accomplished is that of regime change. Saddam Hussein, the Butcher of Baghdad, "now sits in a cell," as Bush said with great satisfaction. The tyrant's sons are dead, his Ba'ath Party fragmented and outlawed, and his statue toppled and melted down to make cooking pots.

Still, the goal of regime change requires not just getting rid of the old regime but also installing a new one. At the moment, there's no tenable Iraqi government to which the United States can hand over the reins.

The hand-selected Governing Council has no writ beyond the range of U.S. firepower. The popular leaders of the moment appear to come mostly from the ranks of the mullahs, most of whom favor the formation of an Islamic theocracy. Such a government is likely to be even less receptive to notions of Western modernity than were the secular, if brutal, Ba'athists.

Well, at least the new Iraqi government, whatever form it takes, will not be able to threaten the world with weapons of mass destruction, as Hussein did. And you can't deny that he did that, even if the threats turned out to be hollow and the weapons nonexistent.

Removing the menace posed by Iraqi weapons was the major stated goal of the war. It is evident now that the threat was little more than an artfully crafted hologram, greatly enhanced by misinterpretations of Western intelligence data.

Bush and his men now maintain it matters not whether Iraq had weapons of mass destruction. What does matter, they say, is that we got rid of a dictator who killed and oppressed his own people. This shift of priorities will no doubt alarm our many dictatorial and oppressive allies and trading partners—if they believe for one moment that's it's sincere.

Another goal of the invasion was to advance the overall war on terror declared after the Sept. 11 attacks. The lack of a link between Iraq and al-Qaida did not discourage Bush and Vice President Dick Cheney from conflating the two. Saddam and Osama? Both Arabs, both our enemies—that's close enough! The latest polls show that something like 60 percent of Americans still believe Iraq was somehow responsible for 9/11.

The fact is, the Iraq invasion seriously diverted manpower and resources from the primary post-9/11 mission in Afghanistan. That is the substance of a recent report published by the U.S. Army War College—not exactly a hotbed of peaceniks.

Ah, but what's the difference? Right after the terror attacks on U.S. soil, Bush proclaimed: "The most important thing for us is to find Osama bin Laden. It is our No. 1 priority." Eight months later, he said this: "I don't know where he is and I really don't care. It's not that important. It's not our priority."

So, it's hard to tell exactly where the priorities lie from one day to the next, but it looks like al-Qaida is back on the front burner, at least this week. U.S. and Pakistani troops have been deployed in the mountainous region at the Afghanistan-Pakistan border. The latest dispatches have them tightening the noose not on Osama but on his second-in command, who reportedly might already be dead—or escaped.

Does it matter, ultimately, whether we get Osama or just his chief lieutenant, or either one? Both men are reportedly invaluable to the terrorist organization. But it is the nature of such networks to be decentralized, not to depend on a single leader. Sometimes, the influence of such men is stronger in death and martyrdom than it is when they're alive.

No one within shouting distance of mainstream U.S. politics advocates the abandonment of our missions in Iraq or Afghanistan. We have to rebuild Iraq, if only because we had such a large hand in destroying the place. It's also high time—way past high time, actually—that we invited the United Nations to assist in the transitional administration of the country we conquered. Likewise, we must continue to harry and harass al-Qaida and affiliated terrorist organizations and bring the surviving perpetrators of 9/11 to justice.

While we're at it, we also ought to expend some of our influence and might on the stalled "road map to peace" for the Palestinian-Israeli conflict. Of all the problems in the Middle East, that of the stateless Palestinians has proven to be the most insolvable—the primary recruiting tool for terrorists and a lasting obstacle to regional stability.

It's a worthy goal with a realizable outcome: That would be nice for a change.

Good intentions paved the way to war

IF THERE'S ONE THING POLITICAL CONSERVATIVES HISTORICALLY REGARD WITH great suspicion, it's public policy founded on good intentions.

That's why most of them opposed Lyndon Johnson's War on Poverty, for example. That opposition does not make them pro-poverty. No, they simply doubt the ability of the federal government to lift poor people into the middle class through welfare and job-training programs.

They believe idealism and tax dollars are an ineffective and sometimes counterproductive mixture.

And yet, the current administration, as conservative as any since that of Coolidge, continues to wage a far more destructive and expensive war based on little more than its own good intentions.

President George W. Bush and his people want to establish a pro-Western democracy in conquered Iraq—a stable and prosperous state that will serve as the very model of a modern Arab nation. It will feature freedom of speech and worship for all, not to mention law and order, accessible education and plentiful supplies of food, water and electricity.

Some liberals might argue we lack some of those things right here in the United States, but that's a dispute for another day. No reasonable person could say that such a vision for Iraq is not noble, that it wouldn't be the best thing all around for both Iraqis and Americans.

The question at hand is whether those good intentions of Bush and Dick Cheney will pave the way to a friendly and democratic Iraq or to someplace far more unpleasant. Posing that question does not make one anti-democracy.

About a year ago, a farsighted, nearsighted and still youthful-looking Tribune columnist predicted that the televised toppling of Saddam Hussein's statue in the Baghdad main square would mark the high-water point of the Iraqi adventure. After that, he said, the hard part would begin.

This weekly columnist—ruggedly handsome despite a long life of dissipation—called on Bush and Cheney to invite the United Nations into Iraq for the purposes of creating a transitional civil administration.

Alas, like so much valid information, this vital nugget of intelligence never made it up the chain to the Oval Office. Maybe it just got lost for a while on Condoleezza Rice's desk. Paul Bremer, who heads the occupying forces' civil administration, is only now meeting with U.N. officials, trying to work something out before the self-imposed June 30 deadline.

Before Bremer could get even that far, however, the situation had settled into grim and brutal guerrilla warfare. Nearly a year after Bush smugly declared "an end to major combat," we have—major combat.

The president who once pledged to be a "great uniter" has come through in spectacular if unexpected fashion. Sunni and Shiite Muslims in Iraq are uniting for the first time in centuries, joined by their shared loathing for the infidel invader. The Iraqi resistance is beginning to take on a nationalistic character.

In Afghanistan, where we supposedly won the day more than two years ago, our man Hamid Karzai, the president of the country, has no control outside the precincts of Kabul. In the countryside, the Taliban has reconstituted itself and rival warlords are engaging in pitched battles. Heroin production is at an all-time high.

Hey, it wasn't supposed to be like this! Don't these people know that we're there for their own good? Don't they realize our intentions are honorable and unselfish?

Maybe they'll finally get it if we send more soldiers over there. That seems to be the consensus among powerful people in Washington, D.C.: We must increase the number of troops in the Middle East!

Now, I'm sure these policy-makers mean well, but I really think we ought to take a deep breath and reassess our strategy before we undertake a major troop escalation. I'll remind everyone of this recommendation in a year or so.

Can you hear me now, Condi? Would you pay more attention if I wrote it in code and placed it in a double-secret drop box?

I caught quite a bit of Rice's testimony before the 9/11 commission, and her main lament was that the various intelligence agencies didn't share pertinent information with one another, that their bureaucratic rivalries pose a "systemic problem" that led to tragic lapses.

Correct me if I'm wrong, but isn't Rice the national security adviser? And is it not the national security adviser's mission to cull the relevant intelligence from the disparate agencies, then analyze it and summarize the conclusions for the president?

There are good reasons for intelligence agencies not to share information. Compartmentalization is at the core of the secret world. Without it, espionage and undercover law enforcement operations would be irretrievably compromised.

The National Security Agency was set up for the sole purpose of coordinating the intelligence and connecting the dots. Rice's complaint seems to be that the national security adviser fell down on the job.

Never fear! The NSA plans to hire 7,500 more staffers in the near future. That's a lot of dot-connecters, fly-swatters and silver-bullet seekers.

We know they mean well. Let's hope they also do well.

Prisoner abuse: It's the war, stupid!

MANY ARABS AND OTHER MUSLIMS MUST HAVE HEARD PRESIDENT GEORGE W. Bush's not-quite-contrite apology for the abuse of Iraqi prisoners, coupled with his confusing assurance that Americans really don't do that sort of thing.

It must have been confusing because there are literally thousands of images demonstrating conclusively that Americans have been doing exactly that sort of thing. It was like listening to "Baghdad Bob," the former Saddam spokesperson who loudly would state as fact what everyone knew to be fiction.

Perhaps some Arabs also heard the televised testimony of Defense Secretary Donald Rumsfeld, who purported to accept "full responsibility" but not its natural consequence: resignation from his high office. He also vowed to bring the wrongdoers to justice, but he said the Pentagon would not seek "scapegoats" among the middle and higher ranks of the officer corps.

It might seem to Iraqis that a mere handful of low-ranking enlisted grunts—six or seven face court-martial proceedings—are the ones taking full responsibility.

That perception could change as the inquiry expands. What is less likely to change is the perception of the images themselves.

Arabs are being bombarded with photos and videos showing U.S. soldiers forcing Iraqis to strip, to form pyramids, to masturbate and to simulate oral sex with one another while a woman soldier leers and mugs for the lens. Another infamous picture shows the same woman holding a leash attached to the neck of a naked man curled in a fetal position.

Remember, these are societies that have never experienced the Renaissance, let alone the sexual revolution.

As much as the hardest of hard-shell Baptists, these people believe in covering their nakedness, especially before the opposite sex. To a lot of Iraqis, Americans aren't just occupiers anymore, not even just oppressors. We're sick perverts who film and photograph our women engaging in sadomasochistic abuse of Muslim men.

You might ask, as many have, what could have possessed the jailers at the Abu Ghraib prison to take such inflammatory and compromising pictures of their own illegal acts. Seymour Hersch, who broke the story, reports that the photographs were employed as interrogation tools. The pictures were considered so horribly mortifying, from a Muslim perspective, that it was believed they would break the morale of recalcitrant prisoners.

No one seems to know where this lousy idea came from. Some potential scapegoat up the line, no doubt—but we're not looking for him, are we?

Imagine for a moment how we would feel if the airwaves were clogged with images of Americans undergoing such torment: chained spread-eagled and naked to a bunk with their faces covered by women's panties. You know and I know the red-eyed rage that would erupt across the U.S. political spectrum. Rush Limbaugh would be apoplectic!

And yet last week, the Big Ditto laughed off the photographs as little more than evidence of frat house-style high jinks. The girls and boys were just "having a good time" and needed "to blow some steam off," he said with his trademark chortle. Other neocons joined the chorus.

"If there has been humiliation, it isn't the fault of the West" said Fox News host Cal Thomas. "It is Muslims' fault."

That particular counterspin can only be counterproductive. It lends credence to the fundamentalist Islamic view that ours is a depraved and decadent society in which such things are tolerated, even encouraged. You might recall that President George W. Bush was famous for his pranks back at the ol' Deke House. Ha-ha!

It's certainly no laughing matter to millions of Muslims. Maybe they'll be impressed by the swift punishment that is sure to befall the half-dozen enlisted soldiers who have been accused. It's also possible that many Arabs would be satisfied with nothing less than the coalition turning the suspects over for Iraqi justice.

Isn't that what we'd want?

In a twisted way, maybe Limbaugh and the other abuse apologists have a point. The images of prison abuse, however you look at them, are just a tiny slice of the ugly reality of war—and not the worst slice, either.

War—any war—is all about death and destruction. Violent coercion is the whole point of the exercise, and it certainly gets a lot more brutal than naked pyramids and forced masturbation. If you're a soldier in an occupying army that is fighting a guerrilla insurgency, guarding a prison is probably pretty soft duty compared with a lot of other postings.

Yes, ugly things happen in wars, no matter how lofty the political strategies behind them. Atrocities did occur in Vietnam, on both sides.

It's the war, stupid. And who got us into this unnecessary and possibly unwinnable war? "Full responsibility" devolves on the president, the vice president and the secretary of defense. Or is "accountability" a concept that applies only to welfare mothers?

It's going to be pretty hard at this point to pitch the United States as nothing more than a benevolent liberator. Circumstances have dictated a new policy direction: Clean up the mess and get the hell out.

If I were an Iraqi, that's what I'd want.

Partisan 'truth' irrelevant in face of war

IT WASN'T EVEN TIME FOR MY CHECKUP WHEN I WENT TO THE DOCTOR, complaining of numbness, irritation, chronic flushing and shortness of pants. She looked me over, noting with concern the hollow circles under my bank balance, and pronounced me, clinically, sound as a Euro.

"What's bothering you, my friend," she said, "is Election Year Campaign Fatigue, or EYCF. I'm afraid no cure is possible until the pharmaceutical companies come up with a catchier acronym."

She advised me to apply a poultice of vinegar and sodium pentathol, lie down for two weeks and avoid fatty news analysis.

There must be a lot of it going around these days because I should have built up a considerable tolerance in the three-plus decades I've been following politics. But this is a sickness of a different strain, and those who actually try to keep up with the campaign news encounter an avalanche of information— more data about the presidential candidates than any person could possibly digest.

Some of it consists of smears, most of it is trivial and much of it focuses excitedly on handicapping the race rather than explaining the issues. Every nugget of real, valuable news is accompanied by tons of slag in the form of manipulative "analysis." For a lot of people, it comes down to John Kerry's Patrician Dignity versus President George W. Bush's Tex Appeal.

The confusion was highlighted in a recent Time magazine article titled "Red Truth, Blue Truth." The concept represents an appalling copout by Time, although it is no doubt valid regarding some issues. Opposing views of abortion rights, for example, spring from fundamentally different premises regarding life and liberty, so there is no common ground but only a fault line.

If you absolutely must cut down on your information overload, forget about the economy, social issues, education and the environment and pay close attention to Iraq. It is the overriding issue in this election, and no shellac of self-serving spin can obscure the ugliness and cruelty of occupation and insurgency.

Not that they don't try. This administration constantly quotes hopeful statistics about new schools and sewer lines. Now, those things are great, don't get me wrong, but please, next time send the Peace Corps! Oh, that's right—it's a wasteful government program.

The news just gets grimmer and more desperate every day. Insurgent factions are forming new alliances to oppose U.S. forces. It just came out that the top U.S. commander in Iraq complained almost a year ago that our troops lacked the supplies to do the job. One of our own transport units last week refused a direct order on the grounds that the assignment was "a suicide mission" into hostile territory. And this is a country we were supposed to have liberated.

Are we in a quagmire yet? It sure quacks like a quagmire.

It's been about 40 years since we deployed significant troops to Vietnam, accompanied by the very best of intentions and the bravest rhetoric: freedom, democracy, open markets and all the rest. The trouble was, no matter how much blood and treasure we invested, we could not control any areas outside Saigon and a few other cities—even though we built schoolhouses even faster than we burned them down.

By the time the futility of the mission became clear, our "national honor" was involved, not to mention our "international credibility." You'd think presidents might pay heed to honor and credibility before they go to war, not just when they're desperate for an exit strategy. But Lyndon Johnson and Richard Nixon continued the conflict because they didn't want to be portrayed as "losing" Vietnam, and tens of thousands of people died in the years it took to work out those sticking points.

The civilized world holds its breath to see whether the United States will make the same mistake again.

The election of John Kerry offers our best chance by far to make a relatively graceful exit from Iraq—a new start with plenty of international face-saving cover, diplomacy instead of brute force and perhaps even, in the end, a stable and not-too-hostile Iraqi regime.

Even assuming the rosiest scenario, Kerry's political foes will no doubt accuse him of "losing" Iraq, which they'll swear would have become another Switzerland if Bush had been left in charge.

President Kerry, if there is one, will be under a lot of pressure to "win" the Iraq war. In this matter I believe he will not waver.

Iraq elections offer hope, not guarantee

Like every patriotic American, I spent the run-up to the Iraqi elections with my fingers crossed, my toes curled and my glutei tightly clenched.

Also my mouth shut, for the most part, because I share President George W. Bush's hope—if not his conviction—that the elections will form the basis for an exit strategy from a military occupation that is proving mutually ruinous.

And like the president, I believe in the transforming power of democracy—the defining idea of Western political thought—at least, most of the time. As Woodrow Wilson confidently predicted, "We're going to teach the Mexicans to elect good men." Elections are not necessarily a panacea, and Americans would be well-advised not to harbor lofty expectations for democracy in Iraq.

South Vietnamese presidents Diem and Thieu and Minh, you might recall, were elected by comfortable margins, or so we were told at the time. The U.S. secretary of defense said in 1964 that we wanted South Vietnam only to be free.

"We do not require that it serve as a Western base or as a member of a Western Alliance," he wrote. "South Vietnam must be free, however, to accept outside assistance as required to maintain its security. This assistance should be able to take the form not only of economic and social measures but also police and military help to root out and control insurgent elements."

He wrote that nearly 10 years before the last U.S. personnel were airlifted off the embassy roof in Saigon.

Iraq is particularly stony soil for democracy, and not because its people are incapable of self-rule. Its borders, to begin with, are arbitrary boundaries imposed long ago by European powers with their own best interests at heart. By now, any half-alert American knows Iraq is about 60 percent Shiite Muslim, with the rest of the population split pretty evenly between Sunnis and Kurds—all historically antagonistic groups. It's hardly the ideal recipe for stable majority rule with respect for minority rights. Was there a foul British plot afoot, hatched over sherry and cigars, to keep Arab nations weak, divided and rent by intertribal warfare? Well, maybe.

Much has been written about the fact that four of Iraq's 18 provinces were too insecure for the elections. The administration has taken a glass-is-three-quarters-full attitude, although the four anarchic provinces were among the nation's most populous. It would be like a U.S. election without Ohio, Florida, Texas, California and Illinois. Gee, in 45 out of 50 states, the voting went just fine. ...

Still, let us assume the process will give a roughly accurate reflection of the Iraqi people's will. Perhaps I didn't follow the campaign as closely as I should have, but I don't remember any of the Iraqi political parties stumping on the platform "Let's keep the occupation going!" The trend seemed to be more along the lines of "Iraq for the Iraqis." If the successful candidate tries to make good on that pledge, it could pose problems for U.S. policy.

Suppose, for example, that the democratically elected Iraqi government decided to renationalize certain industries such as, say, concrete. Iraq used to have a huge concrete industry, thanks largely to the ready availability of crucial materials, namely rock and sand. U.S. occupation policy has been to cut production at these state-owned factories or close them altogether until private capital investors come along.

The expected flood of foreign capital never arrived, so the factories are locked, unemployment is rampant and concrete must be imported at lavish cost. The situation has greatly hindered the rebuilding from the rubble of a new Iraq.

The new government might want to get those factories open, get Iraqis working again, bring in an infusion of revenue and kick-start, finally, the U.S.-funded reconstruction. How sensible!

But I doubt the Bush administration would favor any plan that allowed U.S. tax dollars to be spent on socialist concrete. To them, that would mean the sacrifice of blood and treasure would have been in vain.

Imagine an Iraqi government that would simply order the United States to go home: Pack up, leave immediately and don't trip over the petroleum pipeline on your way out. The request would not be seriously entertained for a moment at the White House or the Pentagon. There are hints that those people aren't really seeking an exit strategy at all but instead an expansion strategy.

That request will never be made, however, because the fledgling government is going to need our help to quell the continuing insurgency. Here, too, is a danger. Before long, we might be asking our ground troops to differentiate between subduing a lawless rebellion and repressing politically restive populations. That can be a difficult line to draw.

Fortunately, our leaders claim to be blessed with great clarity and the ability to draw obvious and unambiguous lines. They draw lines in the sand—lines that shift with the wind, that slide and blur and disappear when disturbed by real-world events.

Forward, into the quagmire!

CHAPTER 7

THE LAST WORD

Is moral relativism ever OK?

IN MY LINE OF WORK, YOU GET TAGGED WITH A LOT OF LABELS—MOST OF THEM unflattering—and one that has been commonly stuck on me is that of "moral relativist."

For a long time, I was unsure of the meaning. But having rarely been accused of anything moral, I was happy to let what I thought to be praise wash over me in warm waves. The tone of the messages implied something altogether different, however, so reluctantly, I looked up the term.

Moral relativism, it turns out, refers to the view that there are no absolute standards of right and wrong, that all such things are based on cultural context and individual outlook.

We of liberal political stripe are apparently awash in moral relativism, unable to entertain or accept "annoying questions about moral absolutes and unacceptable behavior," to quote Bill O'Reilly, the noted cable television ethicist and loofah fantasist.

Furthermore, moral relativism and belief in Darwinian evolution "go hand-in-hand," according to a Web site devoted to the subject. "Evolution teaches that life is accidental, without meaning or purpose. Therefore, anything you do is OK, because it ultimately doesn't matter."

That association might make sense to some people, but they must be acquainted with a whole different set of Darwinians than the ones I know. For the most part, the members of my gang are personally pretty fusty. They're hardly licentious, anyway.

It seems to me that if moral relativism is going to be associated with any particular political mindset, the American right wing is as likely a candidate as any. That possibility dawned when I recently received a missive from a conservative reader that began: "I condemn torture, but ..."

His exception to the no-torture rule was predictable: When our armed forces and intelligence operatives require information from suspected Islamic terrorists, anything goes. After all, these guys are notoriously tough nuts to crack!

Even if the writer is correct, the statement certainly indicates a high degree of moral relativism. Either you condemn torture or you don't.

If there is a middle ground, no one has explored it more thoroughly than Alberto Gonzales, nominee for the post of U.S. attorney general. As John Ashcroft's assistant, Gonzalez wrote the famous "torture memo" that described the Geneva Conventions as "quaint" and said that for something to qualify as torture, "it must be equivalent in intensity to the pain accompanying serious physical injury such as organ failure, impairment of bodily function or even death."

By these strict standards, would something like the simple yanking out of a thumbnail qualify as torture? What about burning someone with a lit cigarette or beating them on the soles of their feet? And is there ever a time, one senator asked Gonzales, that our interrogators are justified in meting out torture?

"I don't believe so," he replied, "but I'd want to get back to you on that."

That answer seems to be morally relativistic—or maybe just exceedingly lawyerly.

At any rate, examples of moral relativism abound in our national politics. If our public officials can't even manage an outright condemnation of something as indisputably vile as torture, what else can we expect?

Some folks think abortion is always wrong. At the same time, a lot more people think that in certain cases, such as a pregnancy caused by incestuous rape, abortion is not the most reprehensible course of action.

It often boils down to the old adage that there are at least two sides to every question. For example, almost everyone believes it's wrong to run a persistent, huge federal budget deficit, but as a Republican politician recently lamented: "People need to remember that to balance the federal budget on the backs of the poorest people in the country is simply unacceptable. You don't pull feeding tubes from people. You don't pull the wheelchair out from under the child with muscular dystrophy."

In matters of public policy, it seems, there are rarely absolute rights and wrongs. You can say slavery, for instance, is always wrong—but it does help to keep down the price of Chinese imports, so we tolerate it. You can unequivocally condemn the taking of innocent civilian lives. Still, a certain amount of "collateral damage" can be expected no matter how noble the cause in which the bombs are dropped.

The more thoroughly you examine the question, the more it appears that all humankind is doomed to a certain measure of moral relativism, although not everyone is ready to admit it. I guess I'll have to acknowledge that I, too, am a moral relativist.

The best I can do is try to be a relatively moral one.

Forgotten lessons of the 20th century

WHEN IT COMES TIME FOR TOMORROW'S HISTORIANS TO POLISH THEIR PINCE-NEZ and put a name to this era in U.S. history, what will they call it?

The day-to-day headlines are pretty depressing: a ruinously expensive and open-ended military occupation; the rending of gigantic holes in the social safety net; science trumped by sanctimony; eye-popping budget deficits; professors hounded for propounding unpopular ideas. ... Also, the polar icecaps are melting.

It usually takes a considerable lag before some prominent historian comes up with a name that sticks, like the McCarthy Era of the 1950s or the Red Scare of the 1920s. It might be decades before we get a definitive tag for the times we live in.

Personally, I lean toward The Blunder Years, but that displays my unscholarly bias. Perhaps it could be called The Time of Forgetting, or the Amnesia Era, because it does seem as though our blessed nation has forgotten or is ignoring the lessons learned during the 20th century.

We might be doomed to learn them all over, and again we'll have to learn them the hard way.

For example, if the Great Depression taught us anything it was the folly of placing our faith in the stock market to ensure the safety of old-age pension funds. Almost everyone, including President George W. Bush, agrees Social Security has been a hugely successful program. Indeed, the current controversy revolves around how best to keep it going.

Bush would destroy Social Security to save it. He proposes a radical redesign that would defeat the whole point of the program, which is not that some people or more people do very well but that no person is left with nothing.

His revamp also calls for trillions of dollars in additional borrowing. Future generations had better hope they get those fabulous returns he promises from their retirement portfolios, because they're going to need that money to pay off the debt we leave them.

Another lesson of the 20th century concerned the value of collective security. World War II was fought to free Europe from the Nazi nightmare and because the Japanese bombed Pearl Harbor.

In the postwar world envisioned by Franklin Roosevelt and Winston Churchill, all nations—democracies and despotisms alike—would attempt to work out their conflicts by diplomatic means under the auspices of the United Nations. Under the rule of law, pre-emptive warfare would be forbidden.

It's fair to say the UN has been less than perfect. Nevertheless, without it the great powers probably would have incinerated one another at some point in the last half-century. Through its work in health, charity and education as well as diplomacy, the organization has saved more lives and eased more international crises than anyone can count.

And yet many neoconservatives are convinced it hasn't been worth the candle. To them, the UN presents an obstacle to the rightful place of the United States as a global imperial power. To my way of thinking, the UN provided the means for America to become an unrivalled superpower, and to discard it would be dangerous. We'll have to let the historians decide.

I thought we also learned in the 20th century that it's wrong to keep people down on the basis of race and ethnicity. World War II was partly about that, too, and so was the civil rights movement. But the Voting Rights Act of 1965 is being dismantled piece by piece through measures such as radical redistricting, which dilutes overall black voting clout even as it ensures a few black-majority congressional districts.

Voter access is becoming more difficult as the administration conjures up a bogeyman of widespread voting fraud: Better 100 people not vote than for one person to vote twice!

Some provisions of the Voting Rights Act are due to expire this year; for example, the requirement that bilingual voting information be made available. Do you think Bush will move to make those provisions permanent, as he has the tax cuts for the richest of us? Nope, that lesson didn't take.

A hundred years ago, quadrupeds were still the main mode of local transportation, and the resources of the Earth still seemed limitless. The 20th century enabled humankind to exploit those resources like never before, with everything from the light bulb to space travel. It also taught us resources are finite, species are fragile and habitat is precious. This concept of environmental stewardship, like so many other breakthroughs, is increasingly considered quaint and irrelevant—disposable, if you will.

A landmark of 20th century jurisprudence was the famous Scopes trial, in which a Tennessee schoolteacher was hauled up on charges of teaching the facts of evolution to impressionable children. The eloquent defense by Clarence Darrow established the principle that biology is backed up by facts, religion by faith, and that the former, not the latter, properly belongs in the classroom.

It appears we'll have to learn that lesson all over again, too, because politicians across the country are mandating the inclusion of creationist theories—such as the sneakily pseudo-scientific "intelligent design"—in public school curricula. It won't be long before some stubborn pedagogue is called on the carpet for refusing to instruct her students in such imbecilities.

It's sad that Ward Churchill, a professor of ethnic studies at the University of Colorado, stands a good chance of becoming an iconic figure of this period in history. He recently gained notoriety for his likening of the capitalist technocrats in the Twin Towers to "little Eichmanns." For this ill-chosen and inflammatory analogy, Churchill is in danger of losing his job.

He is one of those people on university campuses whose job is to spout radical ideas, to throw off sparks, to confront students with completely different ways of seeing the world. The idea—and it's a valid one—is that familiarity with strange perspectives contributes to greater overall understanding, knowledge and wisdom.

Unfortunately, the professors who hold such sinecures are often arrogant, flamboyant and loud—and tenured. Churchill, with his fey ponytail and dubious claim to Native American ancestry, appears to be a typical specimen. If he is fired, which I doubt, there will be another and better gig as an academic provocateur waiting for him. Haven't we learned that lesson? Please, let's not make a martyr of this blowhard!

Supposedly, we also learned a lesson from Vietnam. Begun under spurious pretenses, it dragged on for a decade as a counterinsurgency with no exit strategy other than a fruitless search for an elusive "peace with honor."

And in the end, the Vietnam War didn't defeat communism—not even in Vietnam. What did finish communism as a global force was the Soviet Union's ill-advised pre-emptive invasion of a Muslim country.

But that's a lesson for another day—or another century.

A LIFE IN MUSIC

Ever since I first beat my spoon on the high chair, I wanted to be a performer.

—Forrest Rose

Music is nothing separate from me. It is me ... You'd have to remove the music surgically.

—Ray Charles

Good music is good no matter what kind of music it is.

—Miles Davis

A Life In Love With Music

MANY COLUMBIANS KNEW FORREST ONLY AS A COLUMNIST AND NOTHING about his life as a musician. Some followed his 30-year musical career, but not his columns. A greater number, however, knew his prowess with the pen was rivaled only by his deftness on his beautiful snake-head bass.

Although he made his living as a writer, music was his greatest passion. He was never happier than when thumping that big bass alongside his band mates and cracking jokes in front of an appreciative crowd of friends and fans. Likewise, I was never happier than when I listened to him play. There's something undeniable about watching someone you love do *what* he loves.

Getting the chance to share my life with Forrest during his last five years has been the greatest gift of my middle age. More interesting asleep than most people are awake, he never ceased to awe me. His brilliant mind, razor-sharp wit, and writing and musical talents were rivaled in scope, perhaps, only by his lust for life, generous heart, and playful and loving nature.

Part of that generosity included sharing with me his love of music. Whenever he knocked on my door, he almost always was carrying a CD or old album he thought I'd like—along with a little present he'd picked up somewhere during the day. Some of my fondest memories of our time together were nights on my porch—having a glass of wine and listening to our favorite music. He made me love Joseph Spence, Wayne Hancock and Lefty Frizzell, and I made him crazy for Johnny Hartman, Louis Prima and Anita O'Day. Usually, sometime before the night was over, he'd sing a few verses to one of the seemingly thousands of songs he knew from the great American songbook of country, old-time, bluegrass, blues or jazz. Our nightcap was usually a dance or two around the living room floor.

The collection of tunes included on the CD within cuts a mighty swath across his colorful career, as well as musical genre, and represents so well the Forrest many of us knew and loved. He embraced all kinds of music, and had such a good time playing across the boundaries. It is some small consolation to those who loved him that he spent his last hours playing music he loved with good friends.

The opening tune—*Public Domain*, written by Lee Ruth and performed by The Rank Sinatras—is a rollicking tribute to musicians everywhere and their undeniable influences upon each other. The other bookend, *Take This Hammer*, written by Huddie "Leadbelly" Ledbetter and performed by The Boxbeaters, is a song about freedom from life's shackles. The tunes in between are an eclectic mix of old-time, bluegrass, folk, blues, zydeco, rock and swing.

Most of the recordings were done in studios, but others are from tapes of radio broadcasts and live shows. The latter captures some of Forrest's wonderful emcee spontaneity, his hearty laugh and his inimitable sense of humor and timing. *Public Domain*, *I'm an Old Cowhand*, *Walking in My Sleep* and *S.A.V.E.D* feature him on vocals. The rest pay tribute to his agility on the double bass. To hear him sing the finger-pointing, holier-than-thou *S.A.V.E.D* is a sweet delight; close your eyes and he's right in front of you on The Blue Note stage. The same goes for his superb bass thumping on *Marmaduke's Hornpipe*. Few of us who were regulars at the wildly popular Rank Sinatras' Mojo's-on-the-deck shows will ever forget his rendition of *I'm an Old Cowhand*. He sang it as if Johnny Mercer wrote it for him.

The last number—*The Forrest Rose*—is a beautiful waltz written by St. Louis musician Vince Corkery to honor his friend.

I hope all these songs make you dance and sing and raise a glass to the shining star that was—and is—our Forrest.

—Bernadette Dryden
July 2006

A special thanks to John Stewart for guiding my hand in the compilation of this CD. His longtime friendship with Forrest and many of the musicians made a formidable task a little less so.

A Life in Music 1971-2005

Forrest was a member in the following bands:

Iowa City High School Orchestra *(1971-74)*

Creekside Trio *(1973-74)*
Steve Wine
(this duo played Kingston Trio tunes)

Skunk River Ramblers *(1975)*
Charlie Leslein, Joe Peterson, Pat Schroder

The Mid-Missouri Hellband *(1975-81)*
Mike Fleming, Gary Hunt, Greg Hunt, Mike
Henderson, Marc Rennard, Mike Tonya

High-school practice

Rooster Creek Boys *(guest on KFAL radio show from late '70s-early 2000s)*
Kyle Brown, Bob Hagan, Harold Leake, Ron Lutz, Mark Olson, Russel Orchard,
Clyde Padget, George Rutherford, Dennis Schubert, Gary Sparks

The New Silver Trailer Boys *(early '80s)*
Mike Fleming, Mike Henderson,
Mike O'Neill

The Trailer People *(early '80s)*
Mike Henderson, Denise Landsford,
Mike O'Neill

Boone County Snake Chasers *(1981)*
John Murdock, John G. Stewart

Joe Peterson and Forrest 1975

The Boone County Snakehandlers *(1984-86)*
Chris Brashear, Mike Henderson

**Played and recorded with Taylor McBaine
and John G. Stewart**
(mid '80s)

**Fiddlin' Possum
Walden and the
Musical Marsupials**
(mid '80s)
John G. Stewart,
Charlie Walden

Rockin' Tailfins *(1985)*
Rick Carter,
Deke Dickerson

The Mid-Missouri Hellband

The New Moon Serenaders

Jim Curley

The Boxbeaters
(1985-86)
Mike Henderson,
Dave Pruitt,
Annie Ruh

Kenny Baker
(1985-86)
Bob Black,
Al Murphy

**The New Moon
Serenaders**
(1985-86)
Margaret
Bianchetta, Mary Dee Brown, Annie Ruh, John G. Stewart

Cousin Curtis and the Cash Rebates *(1985-2005)*
Lindell Blackford, Curtis Buckhannon, Dennis Buckhannon, Emily Buckhannon,
Geoff Seitz

The Wolftones *(1986)*
Chris Brashear, Kyle Brown, Bob Hagan, Mike Soltys

Bill Monroe and the Bluegrass Boys *(1986)*

Beats Workin' *(1986-87)*
Chris Brashear, Dave Pruitt

The Eskimo Moaners *(circa 1990)*
Kyle Brown, Lee Bjorndal,
Coleen Peterson, Joe Peterson

Bad Annie and the Better Brothers
(early '90s)
Annie Ruh, Lee Ruth, Jerome Wheeler

The Chipkickers *(early '90s)*
Lowell Appling, Kyle Brown, John Roach, Charlie Walden

Steve Shelton

1991

Brazilbilly *(Nashville—early '90s)*
Jesse Lee Jones

Played and recorded with Geoff Seitz *(early '90s-2005)*

McGee Creek Connection *(1991-92)*
Lowell Appling, Steve Hatfield, Terry Lease, Rich Schwieter, Randy Smith

The Polecats *(1992-93)*
Kyle Brown, Mike Powers, Charlie Walden

The Buckhannon Brothers *(1992-2005)*
Curtis Buckhannon, Dennis Buckhannon

Mudbugs *(1993-94)*
Steve Andsager, Kyle Brown, Amy Toomsen

Monkey Grip *(late '90s)*
Mick Luehrman, Annie Ruh

Played and recorded with David Olney
(Nashville—1997-98)

Perfect Strangers *(2000-2005)*
Bob Black, Chris Brashear, Peter McLaughlin,
Jody Stecher

Laurie Lewis and Tom Rozum *(2002)*

The Rank Sinatras *(2002-2004)*
Claud Crum, Mike Dulak, Joe Hinkebein

The New Madrid Earthquake *(2002-2005)*
Mike Cherry, Henry Clay, Dave Pruitt

Blue Mule *(2004-2005)*
Joe Aguirre, Henry Clay, Dennis Schubert

Jim Curley

Mudbugs

Jim Curley

The Rank Sinatras

Perfect Strangers

Acknowledgments

Our thanks go to the following, who contributed to the compilation of this book and CD project. They include:

Jim Robertson and Hank Waters at the *Columbia Daily Tribune* for arranging and granting copyright transferal.

Earl, Marilyn, Elise, Cecile, Karen, Miriam and Brennan Rose for editorial contributions.

Jim Curley for his outstanding photographs and, who—because of his enduring close friendship with Forrest—was able to provide valuable information and help in immeasurable ways.

John Trotter for the wonderful Bill Monroe photo, of which Forrest was so proud.

Steve Andsager; Thayne Bradford; Chris Brashear; Kyle Brown; Curtis, Dennis and Emily Buckhannon; Henry Clay; Vince Corkery; Claud Crum; Steve Donofrio; Mike and Lois Fleming; Janet and Mike Henderson; Gary Hunt; KDHX, St. Louis; Terry Lease; Mick Luehrman; New Wave Corp./KOPN; David Olney; Mike O'Neill; Coleen and Joe Peterson; Dave Pruitt; Annie Ruh; Lee Ruth; John and Kay Recob; Geoff Seitz; and John Stewart for their assistance in compiling the CD and/or band career roster by granting permissions to use recorded music, providing photographs and researching three decades of dusty memory-bank files to help fill in names of band personnel.

Mike Robertson for his audio-editing skills.

Richard King for his relentless support of live music and local bands.

Carol Goodnick for unearthing that wonderful Boxbeaters tape among her old-jazz collection.

Karen Grindler, Brock Jones, Peter McCarthy, Jon Poses and Kevin Walsh for helping chase down some trivia.

Karen Hudson for marketing guidance.

Les Fortenberry for putting the whole project into a beautiful visual package—and for the wonderful and touching portrait of Forrest; we will cherish it always.

All our friends and family who gave us encouragement, and all of Forrest's friends and fans who inspired his writing and music throughout the years.

— *Bernadette Dryden and Carol Rose, editors*

FORREST ROSE A Life in Music

1. **THE RANK SINATRAS Public Domain** (Lee Ruth) 3:26
   Everybody's Got Love; the Songs of Lee Ruth (Produced by Steve Donofrio for New Wave Corp./KOPN) *Claud Crum, guitar; Mike Dulak, fiddle and backing vocals; Joe Hinkebein, mandolin and backing vocals; Forrest Rose, bass and lead vocals*

2. **MONKEY GRIP Ain't No Cows in Cowtown** (Mick Luehrman, Don Vannoy) 3:10
   The Full Monkey (Wam Music Productions) *Mick Luehrman, guitar, lead and backing vocals; Forrest Rose, bass; Annie Ruh, violin*

3. **GEOFF SEITZ Marmaduke's Hornpipe** (Traditional) 2:07
   The Good Old Days Are Here (Oceana Productions) *Geoff Seitz, violin and hand clapping; Jim Nelson, guitar; Forrest Rose, bass*

4. **THE RANK SINATRAS I'm An Old Cowhand** (Johnny Mercer) 3:28
   If it ain't rank, it ain't right ... (R.S. Productions) *Claud Crum, guitar; Mike Dulak, fiddle and backing vocals; Joe Hinkebein, mandolin and backing vocals; Forrest Rose, bass and lead vocals*

5. **COUSIN CURTIS AND THE CASH REBATES Iola** (Traditional) 2:54
   KDHX Sampler (Copyright 2004 KDHX St. Louis; used by permission of KDHX St. Louis) *Lindell Blackford, mandolin; Curtis Buckhannon, mandolin; Dennis Buckhannon, guitar; Emily Buckhannon, fiddle; Forrest Rose, bass*

6. **MICHAEL HENDERSON Nobody's Fault But Mine** (Traditional) 2:34
   Edge of Night (Produced by Michael Henderson—Dead Reckoning Records) *Michael Henderson, National steel-guitar and mandolin; Kieran Kane, bass drum; Forrest Rose, bass*

7. **PERFECT STRANGERS Homeless Joe** (Chris Brashear) 3:49
   Perfect Strangers (Rebel Records) *Chris Brashear, fiddle, guitar and lead vocal; Jody Stecher, mandolin and tenor vocal; Bob Black, banjo and baritone vocal; Peter McLaughlin, lead guitar; Forrest Rose, bass*

8. **NEW MADRID EARTHQUAKE Lovin' Place** (Henry Clay Ransburgh) 3:44
   New Madrid Earthquake (Produced by Henry Clay and Stephen Gardner) *Henry Clay, vocals and harp; Dave Pruitt, guitar; Forrest Rose, bass; Mike Cherry, drums; Peter Szolka, piano*

9. **THE BUCKHANNON BROTHERS Mexicali Rose** (J. Tenney, H. Stone) 2:44
   Back Home Again (Produced by the Buckhannon Brothers) *Curtis Buckhannon, mandolin; Forrest Rose, bass; Dennis Buckhannon, guitar*

10. **DAVID OLNEY Little Bit of Poison** (David Olney) 3:27
    Through a Glass Darkly (Rounder Records) *David Olney, guitar and vocals; Pat McInerney, percussion; Forrest Rose, bass; Mike Fleming, banjo; AC Bushnell, fiddle*

11. **TAYLOR MCBAINE On The Right Cheek** (Traditional) 1:37
    Boone County Fiddler (Produced by John G. Stewart—Missouri State Old Time Fiddle Association) *Taylor McBaine, fiddle; Forrest Rose, bass; John G. Stewart, guitar*

12. **THE MID-MISSOURI HELLBAND I Know You Rider** (Traditional) (6:46)
    Recorded by Bob Pruitt—The Land Recording Studio, circa 1980 *Mike Fleming, banjo and backing vocals; Mike Henderson, guitar and lead vocals; Gary Hunt, Dobro and backing vocals; Greg Hunt, drums; Forrest Rose, bass*

13. **MUDBUGS I Want to Play With Your Poodle** (Wilson "Boozoo" Chavez) 2:11
    Recorded at Mike Robertson's house, 1993 *Steve Andsager, guitar and vocals; Amy Toomsen, violin and backing vocals; Forrest Rose, bass and backing vocals*

14. **THE NEW SILVER TRAILER BOYS Walking in My Sleep** (Bill Clifton) 2:19
    Produced by the Radio Ranger for KOPN Radio; live broadcast in the KOPN studio, circa 1981 *Mike Fleming, banjo; Mike Henderson, mandolin; Mike O'Neill, guitar; Forrest Rose, bass and lead vocals; Pat O'Connor, snare/brushes*

15-20. **THE BOXBEATERS**
   15. **Sail Away** (R. Newman) 4:52   16. **Rocky Road Blues** (Bill Monroe) 4:31
   17. **Chattanooga Choo Choo** (Harry Warren, Mark Gordon) 4:21   18. **S.A.V.E.D** (Walter Bailes) 4:17   19. **They All Ask'd For You** (The Meters) 4:05   20. **Take This Hammer** (Huddie "Leadbelly" Ledbetter) 3:21
   Recorded at The Blue Note, 1985 *Mike Henderson, National steel-guitar, mandolin and lead vocals on 15, 16, 20; Dave Pruitt, guitar, backing vocals and lead vocals on 17, 19; Forrest Rose, bass, backing vocals and lead vocals on 18; Annie Ruh, violin and backing vocals*

21. **THAYNE BRADFORD The Forrest Rose** (Vince Corkery) 3:18
    Memories for Another Day (Produced by Vince Corkery) *Thayne Bradford, fiddles; Bob Breidenbach, Dobro; Vince Corkery, bass and guitar*

Illustration of Forrest bowing the snake-head bass by Les Fortenberry
CD produced by Bernadette Dryden and John G. Stewart; Mike Robertson, post-production engineer